ASHES TO FIRE

YEAR B

DAILY REFLECTIONS FROM ASH WEDNESDAY TO PENTECOST

EDITED BY
MERRITT J. NIELSON

BEACON HILL PRESS
OF KANSAS CITY

Copyright 2011 by Beacon Hill Press of Kansas City

ISBN 978-0-8341-2762-3

Printed in the
United States of America

Cover Design: Doug Bennett
Interior Design: Sharon Page

Photos from Crosiers: pp. 10, 20, 34, 46, 60, 72, 84, 98, 110, 122, 136, 148, 160, 172, 184
—Gene Plaisted, O.S.C./The Crosiers

Library of Congress Cataloging-in-Publication Data

Ashes to fire Year B devotional : daily reflections from Ash Wednesday to Pentecost / edited by Merritt J. Nielson.
    p. cm.
  Includes bibliographical references.
  ISBN 978-0-8341-2762-3 (hardcover)
  1. Bible—Meditations. 2. Church year meditations. 3. Common lectionary (1992). Year B. I. Nielson, Merritt J., 1945-
BS491.5.A84 2011
  242.8—dc23

                              2011027386

10 9 8 7 6 5 4 3 2 1

CONTENTS

YOU ARE GOD*

(Te Deum Laudamus)

You are God: we praise you;
You are the Lord: we acclaim you;
You are the eternal Father:
All creation worships you.
To you all angels, all the powers of heaven,
Cherubim and Seraphim, sing in endless praise:
Holy, holy, holy Lord, God of power and might,
heaven and earth are full of your glory.
The glorious company of apostles praise you.
The noble fellowship of prophets praise you.
The white-robed army of martyrs praise you.
Throughout the world the holy Church acclaims you;
Father, of majesty unbounded,
your true and only Son, worthy of all worship,
and the Holy Spirit, advocate and guide.
You, Christ, are the king of glory,
the eternal Son of the Father.
When you became man to set us free
you did not shun the Virgin's womb.
You overcame the sting of death
and opened the kingdom of heaven to all believers.
You are seated at God's right hand in glory.
We believe that you will come and be our judge.
Come then, Lord, and help your people,
bought with the price of your own blood,
and bring us with your saints to glory everlasting.
Amen.
*BCP

PREFACE

A Journey with Jesus from Ash Wednesday to Pentecost

*A*shes to Fire is an intentional journey with Jesus from Ash Wednesday through Holy Week and Easter and on to Pentecost Sunday—*from penitence to praise to power*. Central to the Ashes to Fire experience is this daily devotional guide—the *Ashes to Fire Year B Devotional*—a combination of Scripture reading, prayer, corporate worship, small-group Bible study, and personal journaling.

Using the Scripture readings from Year B of the *Revised Common Lectionary*, a devotional reflection based on the Sunday Gospel passage begins each week and serves as the main content for Sunday school and small groups. Daily readings—Monday through Saturday—come from the Old and New Testaments and are accompanied with prayers and spiritual insights from men and women of faith who have helped to form, and continue to shape, our Christian tradition. Graphics and music written specifically for the Ashes to Fire journey provide personal inspiration and spiritual enrichment.

Enhancing this devotional guide are additional resources for worship services and small-group meetings or Sunday school classes. The total Ashes to Fire experience encourages entire congregations—children, youth, and adults—to engage the same passages of Scripture in Christian proclamation, education, and faith formation. This spiritual adventure has already inspired thousands of Christians in hundreds of congregations in a quest for personal and corporate renewal.

Like Christians of earlier eras, we often find ourselves hungering to know God more deeply and intimately. One of the best ways to satisfy that hunger is to immerse ourselves in the Sacred Scriptures. John, in remembering the words of Jesus, gives us a key insight: "You search the scriptures because you *think* that *in them* you have eternal life; and it is they that testify on my behalf"

(John 5:39, emphasis added). When we immerse ourselves in the Written Word, we hear it testify to the Living Word and find ourselves in an ever-deepening relationship with Jesus. In this devotional guide you will discover a breadth and depth of Bible reading, spiritual reflection, and prayer that could, if faithfully followed, inspire the transforming, life-renewing experience with Christ for which your heart hungers.

While you will find the companion resources for the Ashes to Fire experience at www.ashestofire.com and in the Ashes to Fire media kit available from the publisher, remember that this devotional guide is the heart and soul of the journey. Here are the compass points for those who want to join others on this pilgrimage and rehearse with them the stories of our shared faith.

THE LENTEN AND EASTER SEASONS

The season of Lent begins with Ash Wednesday and continues for six weeks. Palm Sunday, the sixth Sunday of Lent, marks the beginning of Holy Week, which includes Maundy Thursday, Good Friday, and Holy Saturday, the day before Easter/Resurrection Sunday. The first Sunday of Easter marks the beginning of the season of Easter, fifty days that lead up to Pentecost Sunday. In total, these fourteen weeks will give shape and substance to this faith adventure. We will gather together as the people of God around fourteen Gospel stories that become the touchstones for reflection, study, and proclamation. During the week, expanded readings in the Gospels will put us in touch with the One to whom they testify—Jesus of Nazareth, the Christ.

Using the *Ashes to Fire Year B Devotional*

THE LENTEN PRELUDE

Ash Wednesday begins the Lenten season. The devotional reflection for this inaugural day calls the entire congregation together for a "solemn assembly." The appeal comes from the ancient prophet Joel, who urges God's people to be contrite and repentant. This day sets the tone for the start of our faith adventure. We reflect on Joel's words: "'Give me your hearts. Come with fasting, weeping, and mourning. Don't tear your clothing in your grief, but tear your hearts instead.' Return to the Lord your God, for he is merciful and compassionate" (Joel 2:12-13, NLT). This is what we want to hear as we set off on this journey together.

The next three days—Thursday, Friday, and Saturday—follow a pattern of personal daily devotions that will be repeated every weekday during the Lenten and Easter seasons, concluding on the Saturday before Pentecost Sunday.

THE MONDAY THROUGH SATURDAY DEVOTIONAL PAGES

Each day of the fourteen-week period follows a similar pattern consisting of Morning Meditations and Evening Reflections. Four Scripture readings are included per day—one from the Old Testament, one from the Psalms, one from the Epistles, and one from the Gospels. If you do not have time to read these passages in their entirety, each of the first three is summarized for you. It is suggested that you always complete the daily Gospel lesson in its entirety (the Scripture quotations are from the *New Revised Standard Version*).

The Bible readings for each day are not necessarily related thematically, although on some days the Scripture selections seem to speak with one voice. However, throughout the weeks you will be reading substantial portions of particular books of the Bible. For instance, during much of the Lenten season the Epistle of 1 Corinthians is read daily in continuity. On the first Monday of Lent, we begin with Mark 1:1, "The beginning of the good news of Jesus Christ, the Son of God," and continue to track with the second Gospel through most of the entire Lenten and Easter seasons.

We also provide in the daily devotional guides a series of inspirational quotations and reflective prayers from men and women of faith who keep us connected with our shared Christian heritage. These great souls of the church include the early fathers, along with more recent apologists for scriptural Christianity such as Dorothy Sayers, Oswald Chambers, C. S. Lewis, and Dennis Kinlaw.

Each evening an excerpt from the Psalms and a brief prayer provide preludes to nighttime rest and renewal. Once again, many of the prayers are adapted extracts from John Wesley's *Forms of Prayer*. Those prayers are identified with a *JW* icon.

THE SUNDAY DEVOTIONAL REFLECTION PAGES

Each Sunday, a devotional reflection based on a key Gospel narrative or teaching provides a background resource for Sunday school class conversations or small-group study. The reflection expresses what a particular writer thinks about the passage. The purpose of this devotional approach is to encourage your engagement with and response to the same portion of Scripture.

In addition to reading the Gospel narrative and the devotional reflection, you should also read the suggested companion passages, usually one from the

Old Testament, one from the Psalms, and one from the New Testament Epistles. Discussion prompts are intended to enhance your experience with the Gospel reading and encourage your participation in group discussions.

The Reflective Journaling section provides an opportunity for you to record any insights and prayers that arise from the day's study. When the fourteen weeks are completed, the *Ashes to Fire Year B Devotional* will become your personal diary of a very important spiritual journey.

THE ART AND MUSIC OF ASHES TO FIRE

Included with this devotional guide are fourteen freshly minted songs for the Ashes to Fire experience. The music is intended for your inspirational reflection, as well as for use in both corporate and small-group worship settings.

Each week, a piece of artwork focuses on the theme of the Sunday Gospel reading. This year the art features stained-glass windows from throughout the world.

This edition contains all new material—Scripture readings, devotional reflections, prayers, and music—based on Year B of the *Revised Common Lectionary*. Together with its trademark interior graphic design and its leatherette binding, the *Ashes to Fire Year B Devotional* provides a resource that seamlessly integrates the message of the Christian faith and a medium that evokes a sacred reverence for the gospel of Christ into a one-of-a-kind faith-forming experience for the entire church. The ultimate goal is personal spiritual renewal and congregational revival as we set out on our journey and embrace God's loving intention that our "hearts [might be] strangely warmed" (John Wesley) and filled to capacity with the love of God. Perhaps the book you hold in your hands will be the answer to your own soul's longings for a relationship with the Lord that will forever change your life. God be with you, pilgrim. Let's take the journey together.

For the Ashes to Fire Team
Merritt J. Nielson
Curriculum Director

We acknowledge a debt of gratitude to our primary writers for the devotional reflections in this journal: Janet Lanham, Helen J. Metcalfe, Russell F. Metcalfe Jr., Jesse Middendorf, Frank Moore, Rick Power, Jeren Rowell, and Woodie Stevens. Please visit www.ashestofire.com for other resources, including Sunday school and small-group discussion guides for children, youth, and adults; sermon and worship suggestions; and music for public services.

PLEASE NOTE: **This devotional journal is an undated resource. Consult a church calendar or lectionary for specific dates for use during the current year.**

LENTEN SEASON

Ash Wednesday
Call a Solemn Assembly—
The Family Meeting

Read Joel 2:1-2, 12-17, the introductory reflection titled "Call
a Solemn Assembly—The Family Meeting," and then the
additional devotional material for Ash Wednesday on page 16.

THE MUSIC OF ASHES TO FIRE

Prelude Days: "From the Ashes" (Track 1)

Thursday through Saturday

IN THE MORNING:

A personal daily devotional guide includes prayer,
a reading from the Old Testament, the Psalms, the Epistles,
and the Gospel for each day of the week.

The Bible readings for the Lenten Prelude are from Joel,
Habakkuk, Ezekiel, Hebrews, Philippians, and John 17.

Inspirational quotes from men and women of faith
keep us in contact with our shared Christian heritage.

IN THE EVENING:

An evening psalm and prayer become preludes
to nighttime rest and renewal.

LENTEN SEASON—THE PRELUDE
Call a Solemn Assembly—The Family Meeting

A devotional reflection based on Joel 2:1-2, 12-17

I can still picture the scene. The images, smells, and feelings of it are indelibly imprinted upon my mind and heart. The scene was repeated often in the home where I grew up. It usually happened in the dining room, but sometimes it spilled over into the living room at special tables my dad made just for that purpose. It was the celebration of a shared meal. And those kinds of meals at our house were never just meals—they were events.

My mother knew how to throw a party for almost any reason. The major holidays and birthdays were, of course, a given. But there were other events: an engagement, a birth, a job promotion, or a good report card. It may have been for a visiting missionary or a travelling relative. Often it was in celebration of an achievement, and once in a while we were soothing a defeat. Virtually anything worth marking we marked by gathering around the table. They were festive events, and they have become some of the warmest memories I have of childhood.

The purpose was not really the occasion itself. I've forgotten a lot of the reasons we had those meals. The significance was not even in the wonderful food or the special table decorations, though all were splendid. Those meals remain in my consciousness mostly because of what happened after the plates were full and the eating began. There was usually a brief moment when all that could be heard was the tinkling of silverware on the good china. But then it would happen. The stories would begin. That was my favorite part.

From my earliest memory I loved to sit and hear the stories of my family. There were stories of how Mom and Dad met and eventually married. I liked the stories of my grandparents in the rugged days of rural life in Arkansas. My uncles and aunts told stories of how it was during the war. And best of all were stories of the spiritual heritage of our family.

I cannot fully explain it or even completely describe it, but somehow in all that took place around that table something very important happened inside of me. I learned who I was. As we participated in our common memory, I found my place, my name, my story there at the table.

The church wisely assigns this reading from the prophet Joel to begin our Lenten journey. The connection is evident as we hear the exhortation to "sanctify a fast" (v. 15). We know that special times of fasting and prayer are vital for spiritual growth. Undoubtedly many of us have already been thinking about how we might embrace the opportunity we have during this season of the Christian year to draw closer to the Lord. That's an important spiritual objective. Yet if it goes no further than our personal discipline, it remains something less than full-bodied discipleship.

Perhaps our observance of Lenten discipline has become far too individualistic. We tend to ask questions such as, "How will *I* hear from God afresh this season? What should *I* give up during this time of fasting?" Joel's call to repentance and fasting is a call to the entire community. This is to be "family table" time. No one is dismissed, no one is excluded, because what happens during these times is ultimately important and life shaping. So the preacher says, "Assemble the aged; gather the children, even infants" (v. 16).

This is no incidental detail in the call to God's people. The intergenerational nature of the community of faith is essential to faithful worship and witness. Wesleyans ought to be well versed in this truth, for we know, as Wesley wrote in his journal, that "the Bible knows nothing of solitary religion." The focus of the church in recent decades on the benefits of specialized ministry to various age-groups may also have impoverished the robust communal life to which the Scriptures regularly testify. What if a rich experience of Lenten renewal awaits you and the congregation to which you belong as you repent of our atomized contemporary experience and call the community of faith back together?

This possibility raises many important questions. If calling everyone to the family table is an important spiritual discipline, then what might need to be rearranged in your life and in the church you attend during these days? Perhaps this is a good time to rethink the inclusion of children in these annual rhythms of worship.

Are the children ever present when adults rise to give testimony to God's work in their lives? Are the children ever present when the offering is received so they can watch their parents place the family tithe in the offering plate? Do they come to the Lord's Table? Do they gather at the altar with the congregation? Do they ever hear the pastor preach?

Some have protested that these "adult" acts of worship are too far beyond the grasp of a child and that a careful congregation makes everything "kid friendly" and age specific. That's faulty logic. Which of us knows the full meaning of the acts of worship? What we all need to know, regardless of age, is the beautiful experience of the entire congregation gathering to enact its faith.

Intergenerational worship requires some intentional planning and preparation. How can all ages participate in leading the congregation in worship? Children, teens, and adults of all ages should be visibly involved in the acts of the worshipping community. Advance planning can provide special worship activities for children that help them to engage in the components of the service with which they may not be familiar. Worship leaders should think about the language used to create an atmosphere of hospitality.

Whatever the strategies, the Lord's clear call to us as we enter this special time of spiritual discipline is to gather the family at the table. May each of us find in the telling of the greatest of all stories our place, our name, and our sense of belonging in the family of God. —JR

REFLECTIVE JOURNALING

_____

_____

_____

_____

_____

_____

_____

_____

_____

_____

_____

PSALM 103 ▪ JOEL 2:1-2, 12-17 ▪ HEBREW 12:1-14 ▪ LUKE 18:9-14

MORNING MEDITATIONS

PRAYER—Lord God, send your Holy Spirit to be the guide of all my ways and the sanctifier of my soul and body. Give me the light of your presence, your peace from heaven, and the salvation of my soul, through Jesus Christ my Lord. Amen. **JW**

PSALM 103:13-14—As a father has compassion for his children, so the LORD has compassion for those who fear him. For he knows how we were made; he remembers that we are dust.

JOEL 2:12, 15-16a, 17b   *Call a Solemn Assembly*
Yet even now, says the LORD, return to me with all your heart, with fasting, with weeping, and with mourning . . . Blow the trumpet in Zion; sanctify a fast; call a solemn assembly; gather the people . . . Let them say, "Spare your people, O LORD."

HEBREWS 12:7a, 11   *Endure Trials*
Endure trials for the sake of discipline . . . Now, discipline always seems painful rather than pleasant at the time, but later it yields the peaceful fruit of righteousness to those who have been trained by it.

LUKE 18:9-14   *Today's Gospel Reading*

All those who were ministers of the grace of God have spoken, through the Holy Spirit, of repentance. The very Lord of all himself has spoken of it . . . By my life, the Lord declares, it is not the sinner's death I desire, so much as his repentance.

ST. CLEMENT, *LETTER TO THE CORINTHIANS*

EVENING REFLECTIONS

PSALM 130:1-2a, 3-4a—Out of the depths I cry to you, O LORD. Lord, hear my voice . . . If you, O LORD, should mark iniquities, Lord, who could stand? But there is forgiveness with you.

PRAYER—Father, grant me forgiveness of what is past, and a perfect repentance of all my failings that in the days to come I may with a pure spirit, do your will—walking humbly with you, showing love to all, keeping my soul in holiness, and my body in sanctification and honor, in Jesus' name. Amen. **JW**

THURSDAY

PSALM 37 ▪ **HABAKKUK 3:1-18** ▪ **PHILIPPIANS 3:12-21** ▪ **JOHN 17:1-18**

MORNING MEDITATIONS

PRAYER—O God, in my passage through this world, do not let my heart become its slave. But always fix my undivided attention on the prize of my high calling. Let me do this one thing: let me press towards this goal with such zeal that everything I do today will help me reach that goal. Prepare my heart for that pure bliss that you are preparing for all those who love you. Amen. *JW*

PSALM 37:5, 8-9—Commit your way to the LORD; trust in him, and he will act . . . Refrain from anger, and forsake wrath. Do not fret—it only leads to evil. For the wicked shall be cut off, but those who wait for the LORD shall inherit the land.

HABAKKUK 3:17a, 17c-19a *Yet I Will Rejoice*
Though the fig tree does not blossom, and no fruit is on the vines . . . though the flock is cut off from the fold, and there is no herd in the stalls, . . . yet I will rejoice in the LORD; I will exult in the God of my salvation. GOD, the Lord, is my strength.

PHILIPPIANS 3:12, 13b-14 *I Press On*
Not that I . . . have already reached the goal; but I press on to make it my own, because Christ Jesus has made me his own . . . This one thing I do: forgetting what lies behind and straining forward to what lies ahead, I press on toward the goal for the prize of the heavenly call of God in Christ Jesus.

JOHN 17:1-18 *Today's Gospel Reading*

Fast now and you will feast hereafter; weep now and you will laugh hereafter. Present mourning brings future joy . . . The Lord is gracious and merciful, preferring the repentance of the sinner to his death, slow to anger and abounding in steadfast love.

ST. JEROME, *COMMENTARY ON JOEL*

EVENING REFLECTIONS

PSALM 38:9, 21-22—O Lord, all my longing is known to you; my sighing is not hidden from you . . . Do not forsake me, O LORD; O my God, do not be far from me; make haste to help me, O Lord, my salvation.

PRAYER—My Lord and my God, I turn to you in sincerity of heart and, renouncing all self-interest, give myself up entirely to you. I desire to be . . . yours forever. O my Savior and Sanctifier, turn your face to this poor soul . . . and accept the gift of myself. Amen. *JW*

PSALM 31 ▪ EZEKIEL 18:1-4, 25-32 ▪ PHILIPPIANS 4:1-9 ▪ JOHN 17:9-19

MORNING MEDITATIONS

PRAYER—Everlasting God, I bless you with my whole heart and thank you for your goodness to me. Watch over me today with eyes of mercy; direct my soul and body according to your will, and fill my heart with your Holy Spirit that I may live this day, and all the rest of my days, to your glory. Amen. *JW*

PSALM 31:3-5—You are indeed my rock and my fortress; for your name's sake lead me and guide me, take me out of the net that is hidden for me, for you are my refuge. Into your hand I commit my spirit; you have redeemed me, O LORD, faithful God.

EZEKIEL 18:30b-31 *Get Yourself a New Heart*
Repent and turn from all your transgressions; otherwise iniquity will be your ruin. Cast away from you all the transgressions that you have committed against me, and get yourselves a new heart and a new spirit! Why will you die, O house of Israel?

PHILIPPIANS 4:8 *Think On These Things*
Whatever is true, whatever is honorable, whatever is just, whatever is pure, whatever is pleasing, whatever is commendable, if there is any excellence and if there is anything worthy of praise, think about these things.

JOHN 17:9-19 *Today's Gospel Reading*

Because the promise of God that, from mortality and corruption, from this weak and abject state, from dust and ashes, we could become equal to the angels of God seemed incredible to men, he not only made a written covenant . . . but also gave them a Mediator as a pledge of his promise. ST. AUGUSTINE, *DISCOURSES ON THE PSALMS*

EVENING REFLECTIONS

PSALM 35:10, 22—O LORD, who is like you? You deliver the weak from those too strong for them, the weak and needy from those who despoil them . . . You have seen, O LORD; do not be silent! O Lord, do not be far from me!

PRAYER—O God the Father, have mercy upon me. O God the Son, who knowing the Father's will, came into the world to save me, have mercy upon me. O God the Holy Spirit, who for the same purpose sanctified me in baptism and has breathed holy thoughts into me, have mercy upon me. Amen. *JW*

PSALM 30 ▪ EZEKIEL 39:21-29 ▪ PHILIPPIANS 4:10-20 ▪ JOHN 17:20-26

MORNING MEDITATIONS

PRAYER—O Lord of Life, put your grace into my heart, that I may worthily magnify your great and glorious name. You have made me and sent me into the world to do your work. Assist me to fulfill the purpose of my creation, and to show your praise by giving myself to your service, today and always. Amen. *JW*

PSALM 32:5—I acknowledged my sin to you, and I did not hide my iniquity; I said, "I will confess my transgressions to the LORD," and you forgave the guilt of my sin.

EZEKIEL 39:25-27 *They Shall Forget Their Shame*
Therefore thus says the Lord GOD: Now I will restore the fortunes of Jacob, and have mercy on the whole house of Israel . . . They shall forget their shame, and all the treachery they have practiced against me . . . when I have . . . gathered them from their enemies lands, and through them have displayed my holiness.

PHILIPPIANS 4:12-13 *I Can Do All Things Through Christ*
I know what it is to have little, and I know what it is to have plenty. In any and all circumstances I have learned the secret of being well-fed and of going hungry, of having plenty and of being in need. I can do all things through him who strengthens me.

JOHN 17:20-26 *Today's Gospel Reading*

He showed us the way of humility by his counsels and followed it by suffering for us . . . Though he was great, he was humbled. Being humbled, he was put to death. Put to death, he rose again and was exalted . . . He gave us humility as a way. If we follow it, we shall give thanks to the Lord.   ST. AUGUSTINE, *SERMON 23A*

EVENING REFLECTIONS

PSALM 42:1, 2a, 5—As a deer longs for flowing streams, so my soul longs for you, O God. My soul thirsts for God, for the living God . . . Why are you cast down, O my soul, and why are you disquieted within me? Hope in God; for I shall again praise him, my help.

PRAYER—O God, you instruct me with your laws, you redeem me by the blood of your Son, and you sanctify me by the grace of your Holy Spirit. For these and all other mercies, how can I ever worthily love you or magnify your great and glorious name? Forever, I will bless you and adore your goodness. Amen. *JW*

WEEK ONE
Lenten Season

Sunday: Remember Who You Are

Read the Gospel passage from Mark 1:9-15 and the devotional reflection titled "Remember Who You Are," then respond to the discussion prompts in the Reflective Journaling section.

THE MUSIC OF ASHES TO FIRE

Week 1: "God of the Ruins" (Track 2)

Monday through Saturday of Week 1

IN THE MORNING:

A personal daily devotional guide includes prayer, a reading from the Old Testament, the Psalms, the Epistles, and the Gospel for each day of the week.

This week's readings are from Genesis, 1 Corinthians, and the Gospel of Mark.

Inspirational quotes from men and women of faith keep us in contact with our shared Christian heritage.

IN THE EVENING:

An evening psalm and prayer become preludes to nighttime rest and renewal.

LENTEN SEASON–WEEK ONE
Remember Who You Are

A devotional reflection based on Mark 1:9-15

*R*ead the Gospel passage first, then the devotional reflection that follows. The discussion prompts at the end will help prepare you for Sunday school and small-group sessions.

The Bible says, "No temptation has seized you except what is common to man" (1 Cor. 10:13, NIV). What do you suppose would happen in your church if this Sunday each person stood to share in total honesty about the temptations that seized him or her this week? Think we could do it? If we could, we might be amazed to discover that whatever our temptations may be, we are not alone, that indeed temptation is common.

This is probably why long ago the church said, "You know, maybe we need to set aside some time every year when we especially think about spiritual disciplines. Maybe we need to be reminded every year that temptation is common, even for saved and sanctified Christians." So in the fourth century the church began to set aside the forty regular days prior to Easter as a time for this kind of focus. It was particularly a time when new Christians were prepared for their baptisms on Easter Sunday.

Because these new believers would be welcomed into the household of faith, the whole church was called to a time of preparation. It was also a time when those who had become separated from the church could prepare to rejoin the fellowship. Part of the preparation was about taking seriously the reality of temptation in our lives and so the need for fasting and prayer as a way of learning how to resist temptation.

We can see then why this text would come to us on the first Sunday in Lent. The temptation of our Lord Jesus serves as a model for us of how to resist temptation and how to live in obedience. The writer of Hebrews tells us that Jesus was "tempted in every way, just as we are—yet was without sin" (4:15,

NIV). I don't know about you, but that encourages me. Our Lord Jesus knows what it's like to live here.

It is certainly no accident that the story of Jesus being tempted is connected in the Gospels to the story of his baptism by John. Mark tells the baptism story quite simply, but it is no less powerful and the connection to the temptation of Jesus is quick and sharp. Mark says of Jesus that "just as he was coming up out of the water, he saw the heavens torn apart and the Spirit descending like a dove on him" (Mark 1:10). Then "a voice . . . from heaven" spoke and said, "You are my Son, the Beloved; with you I am well pleased" (v. 11).

What a moment! You would think that this kind of confirmation is all Jesus would need to begin his ministry. His identity as the very Son of God has been established in a profound way. What else would he need? And yet Mark says that the Spirit "immediately drove him" into the desert for this time of testing (v. 12). Why?

Could it be that learning to resist temptation is not first about particular acts of spiritual discipline? Perhaps resisting temptation is more about knowing who we are. This wilderness confrontation with the devil will press Jesus most at the point of identity. Is he *really* the Son of God? Will God *really* provide for him and protect him? Right there is the place that temptation gets a foothold in our lives.

When our identity as God's children is questioned, when our value is threatened, when our very survival is in doubt, that's when we are tempted to believe we have to take care of ourselves. In these critical moments a core question must be answered. It's the same question pressing in on Jesus in these encounters with Satan: Who am I? Who will I be? And *whose* will I be? Facing down temptation successfully in our lives has to get deeper than just choosing right from wrong. It has to go down to the core of who we are, to our identity as children of God.

As a teenager when I was getting ready to go out with my friends, my dad had the wisdom to move deeper than trying to remind me of how to act or to give me a list of dos and don'ts. He simply said to me, "Son, remember who you are." After my dad said those words, I went out with my friends, very few of whom professed to be Christians. Sometimes I found myself in situations where I knew I should not be. I was faced with choices and pressures to do things and act in ways I knew were not consistent with life in Christ.

I struggled with those choices. I wanted to fit in and be a part of the group as much as anyone else. The temptation to throw my values to the wind was strong and real. If in those moments all I had been given was a list of rules, it would have been easy to rationalize losing the list. Thankfully I had been given much more than that. I carried with me into those situations an identity, an image of faithfulness rooted in Christ and modeled for me by my parents. Consequently, in the heat of a moment of decision I did not have to say, "Oh, wait a minute. Let me check my list." That likely would never have happened. No, my father didn't just give me a list, he gave me his heart.

This is precisely what God has given to us, and our Lord Jesus models how to access the powerful reality of our identity as the beloved of God. Complete trust in God that keeps us true in the midst of temptation comes from a deep and secure sense of our identity as children of God. And that's really what the spiritual disciplines are about.

This is why we are entering a season of fasting and prayer, this time of putting off some things or of taking on some other things that would draw us closer to God. Maybe for you these days should be about nothing less than offering to God that circumstance of your life that has you down, depressed, and defeated. It does not define you; God's love does.

May these days of the Lenten journey be for you an opportunity to remember who you are, a beloved child of God redeemed by grace. And may this memory establish you in the faith expressed by the apostle: "For I know whom I have believed, and am persuaded that he is able to keep that which I have committed unto him against that day" (2 Tim. 1:12, KJV). —JR

After reading the passage from Mark 1:9-15 and the devotional reflection "Remember Who You Are," you may also want to read the following related passages:

Genesis 9:8-17; Psalm 25:1-10; 1 Peter 3:18-22

The discussion prompts that follow will help prepare you to participate in your Sunday school class or small-group study. Use your Reflective Journaling section to record any other insights that come to you as you read the Gospel lesson and the devotional reflection.

DISCUSSION PROMPT NO. 1: MARK 1

Why do you think God the Father proclaimed Jesus as his Son with whom he is "well pleased" at Jesus' baptism?

DISCUSSION PROMPT NO. 2: MARK 1

Why do you think it was important for Jesus to be baptized and resist temptation before beginning his public ministry?

DISCUSSION PROMPT NO. 3: MARK 1

Describe some ways you have sensed God's love for you as his child.

DISCUSSION PROMPT NO. 4: MARK 1

Why do you think repentance and belief are appropriate responses to the news that the kingdom of God is near? Why is that good news?

DISCUSSION PROMPT NO. 5: DEVOTIONAL REFLECTION

What does it mean to you to be a "beloved child of God redeemed by grace"?

REFLECTIVE JOURNALING

_____

_____

_____

_____

_____

_____

_____

_____

_____

_____

_____

_____

_____

_____

_____

_____

PSALM 52 ▪ **GENESIS 37:1-11** ▪ **1 CORINTHIANS 1:1-19** ▪ **MARK 1:1-13**

MORNING MEDITATIONS

PRAYER—Father in heaven, at the baptism of Jesus in the River Jordan you proclaimed him your beloved Son and anointed him with the Holy Spirit. Grant that all who are baptized into his name may keep the covenant they have made and boldly confess him as Lord and Savior. Amen.

PSALM 52:8b-9—I trust in the steadfast love of God forever and ever. I will thank you forever, because of what you have done. In the presence of the faithful I will proclaim your name, for it is good.

GENESIS 37:5a, 7-8b *Are You Indeed to Reign Over Us?*
Once Joseph had a dream, and . . . he told it to his brothers . . . "There we were, binding sheaves in the field. Suddenly my sheaf rose and stood upright; then your sheaves gathered around it, and bowed down to my sheaf." His brothers said to him, "Are you indeed to reign over us? Are you indeed to have dominion over us?"

1 CORINTHIANS 1:4, 8-9 *God's Grace Has Been Given to You*
I give thanks to my God always for you because of the grace of God that has been given you in Christ Jesus . . . He will also strengthen you to the end, so that you may be blameless on the day of our Lord Jesus Christ. God is faithful; by him you were called into the fellowship of his Son, Jesus Christ our Lord.

MARK 1:1-13 *Today's Gospel Reading*

As soon as the grace of God in the sense of his pardoning love is manifested to our souls, the grace of God as the power of his Spirit is at work within us. And now we can perform, through God, . . . all things in the light and power of that love.   JOHN WESLEY, *SERMON 11*

EVENING REFLECTIONS

PSALM 44:4a, 7-8—You are my King and my God . . . You have saved us from our foes, and have put to confusion those who hate us. In God we have boasted continually, and we will give thanks to your name forever.

PRAYER—O God, give me grace to study your knowledge every day, so that the more I know you, the more I may love you. Create in me a zealous obedience to all your commands, a cheerful patience under your disciplines, and a thankful resignation to your will. Amen. **JW**

PSALM 45 ▪ GENESIS 37:12-28 ▪ 1 CORINTHIANS 1:20-31 ▪ MARK 1:14-28

MORNING MEDITATIONS

PRAYER—Teach us, good Lord, to serve as you deserve; to give and not to count the cost; to fight and not to heed the wounds; to toil and not seek for rest; to labor and not to ask for any reward, except that of knowing that we do your will; through Jesus Christ our Lord. Amen. *St. Ignatius of Loyola*

PSALM 45:6-7a—Your throne, O God, endures forever and ever. Your royal scepter is a scepter of equity; you love righteousness and hate wickedness.

GENESIS 37:26-27, 28b   *They Sold Him for Twenty Pieces of Silver*
Then Judah said to his brothers, "What profit is it if we kill our brother and conceal his blood? Come, let us sell him to the Ishmaelites, and not lay our hands on him, for he is our brother, our own flesh." And his brothers agreed . . . and sold him to the Ishmaelites for twenty pieces of silver.

1 CORINTHIANS 1:27-29   *God Chose What Is Foolish*
God chose what is foolish in the world to shame the wise; God chose what is weak in the world to shame the strong; God chose what is low and despised in the world, things that are not, to reduce to nothing things that are, so that no one might boast in the presence of God.

MARK 1:14-28   *Today's Gospel Reading*

We take up our cross, and deny ourselves every pleasure that does not lead us to God. It is thus that we wait for entire sanctification; for a full salvation from our sins . . . or as the Apostle expresses it, "go on to perfection." But what is perfection? It is love excluding sin; love filling the heart, taking up the whole capacity of the soul.

JOHN WESLEY, *THE SCRIPTURE WAY OF SALVATION*

EVENING REFLECTIONS

PSALM 47:2-3, 7—The LORD, the Most High, is awesome, a great king over all the earth. He subdued peoples under us, and nations under our feet. He chose our heritage for us, the pride of Jacob whom he loves . . . For God is the king of all the earth; sing praises with a psalm.

PRAYER—Lord, I ask that I may look for nothing, claim nothing, and expect nothing but you, and that I may go through all the scenes of life, not seeking my own glory, but looking wholly unto you, and acting wholly for you. Amen. *JW*

PSALM 119:49-72 ▪ GENESIS 37:29-36 ▪ 1 CORINTHIANS 2:1-13 ▪ MARK 1:29-45

MORNING MEDITATIONS

PRAYER—O Lord, govern my life by your wisdom, so that my soul may always be serving you as you desire, not as I may choose. Do not grant what I ask if it offends your love, which must always be living in me. Let me die to myself, that I may serve you; let me live to you, for you are the true life. Amen.

PSALM 119:66-68—Teach me good judgment and knowledge; for I believe in your commandments. Before I was humbled I went astray, but now I keep your word. You are good and do good; teach me your statutes.

GENESIS 37:31, 32b-33a, 36 *The Midianites Sold Joseph*
Then they took Joseph's robe, slaughtered a goat, and dipped the robe in the blood . . . "This we have found; see now whether it is your son's robe or not." [Jacob] recognized it, and said, "It is my son's robe!" . . . Meanwhile, the Midianites sold [Joseph] in Egypt to Potiphar, one of Pharaoh's officials.

1 CORINTHIANS 2:2-4 *Jesus Christ, and Him Crucified*
I decided to know nothing among you except Jesus Christ, and him crucified. And I came to you in weakness and in fear and in much trembling. My speech and my proclamation were not with plausible words of wisdom, but with a demonstration of the Spirit and of power.

MARK 1:29-45 *Today's Gospel Reading*

Christian faith is not only an assent to the whole gospel of Christ, but also a full reliance on the blood of Christ; a trust in the merits of his life, death, and resurrection. We have a sure and constant faith, not only that the death of Christ is available for all the world, but that he has made a full and sufficient sacrifice for *you*, a perfect cleansing of *your* sins.

JOHN WESLEY, *SERMON 5*

EVENING REFLECTIONS

PSALM 49:7—Truly, no ransom avails for one's life, there is no price one can give to God for it.

PRAYER—O God, you are the giver of all good gifts and I desire to praise your name for all of your goodness to me. I thank you for sending your Son to die for my sins, for the means of grace, and for the hope of glory, through Jesus Christ. Amen. *JW*

PSALM 50 ▪ GENESIS 39:1-23 ▪ 1 CORINTHIANS 2:14—3:15 ▪ MARK 2:1-12

MORNING MEDITATIONS

PRAYER—O Lord, I thank you for all your daily blessings, for keeping me through the night, and providing for my health, strength, and comfort. May I always praise your holy name and love you, my Redeemer, in Jesus' name. Amen.

PSALM 50:1-2—The mighty one, God the LORD, speaks and summons the earth from the rising of the sun to its setting. Out of Zion, the perfection of beauty, God shines forth.

GENESIS 39:3-4, 5b   *The Lord Was with Him*
His master saw that the LORD was with him, and that the LORD caused all that he did to prosper in his hands. So Joseph found favor in his sight and attended him; [Potiphar] made [Joseph] overseer of his house and put him in charge of all that he had . . . the LORD blessed the Egyptian's house for Joseph's sake.

1 CORINTHIANS 3:10-11   *The Foundation Is Jesus Christ*
According to the grace of God given to me, like a skilled master builder I laid a foundation, and someone else is building on it. Each builder must choose with care how to build on it. For no one can lay any foundation other than the one that has been laid; that foundation is Jesus Christ.

MARK 2:1-12   *Today's Gospel Reading*

God will do his own work in his own way with different persons. It does not matter whether it takes place in pleasing or painful ways so long as nature is subdued, pride and self-will dethroned, and the will of God done in us and by us. Therefore, do not compare your experience with others. God knows you, and let him do with you as he sees best.

JOHN WESLEY, *A LETTER TO MISS FURLEY*, 1757

EVENING REFLECTIONS

PSALM 19:12b, 14—Clear me from hidden faults . . . Let the words of my mouth and the meditation of my heart be acceptable to you, O LORD, my rock and my redeemer.

PRAYER—O Lord, I want to offer an evening sacrifice, the sacrifice of a contrite spirit. Have mercy on me, O God, according to your great goodness and the multitude of your mercies. Cleanse me from all filthiness of flesh and spirit that I may follow you with a pure heart and mind. Amen. *JW*

PSALM 40 ▪ GENESIS 40:1-23 ▪ 1 CORINTHIANS 3:16-23 ▪ MARK 2:13-22

MORNING MEDITATIONS

PRAYER—I am no longer my own but yours. Put me to what you will, rank me with whom you will; put me to doing, put me to suffering; . . . let me be full, let me be empty, let me have all things, let me have nothing. I freely and wholeheartedly yield all things to your pleasure and disposal. And now, blessed God, Father, Son and Holy Spirit, you are mine and I am yours. Amen. *JW*

PSALM 40:1-2, 11—I waited patiently for the LORD; he inclined to me and heard my cry. He drew me up . . . out of the miry bog, and set my feet upon a rock . . . Do not, O LORD, withhold your mercy from me; let your steadfast love . . . keep me safe forever.

GENESIS 40:21-23 *He Forgot Joseph*
He restored the chief cupbearer to his cupbearing, and he placed the cup in Pharaoh's hand; but the chief baker he hanged, just as Joseph had interpreted to them. Yet the chief cupbearer did not remember Joseph, but forgot him.

1 CORINTHIANS 3:21, 22b-23 *You Belong to Christ*
So let no one boast about human leaders. For all things are yours . . . all belong to you, and you belong to Christ, and Christ belongs to God.

MARK 2:13-22 *Today's Gospel Reading*

Certainly spiritual temptations will pass through your spirit . . . [But] you are a child of God, a member of Christ, an heir of the kingdom. What you have hold fast, and you shall have all that God has prepared for those who love him . . . You cannot live on what he did yesterday. Therefore he comes today . . . to destroy anything that is not of God.

JOHN WESLEY, *LETTER TO MISS MARCH*, 1760

EVENING REFLECTIONS

PSALM 51:15-16a, 17—O Lord, open my lips, and my mouth will declare your praise. For you have no delight in sacrifice . . . The sacrifice acceptable to God is a broken spirit; a broken and contrite heart, O God, you will not despise.

PRAYER—Father, accept my imperfect repentance, have compassion on my infirmities, forgive my faults, purify my uncleanness, strengthen my weakness, and let your good Spirit watch over me forever, and your love ever rule in my heart, through the merits and sufferings and love of your Son, in whom you are always well pleased. Amen. *JW*

PSALM 55 ▪ GENESIS 41:1-45 ▪ 1 CORINTHIANS 4:1-7 ▪ MARK 2:23—3:6

MORNING MEDITATIONS

PRAYER—Take, Lord, all my liberty, my memory, my understanding and my whole will. You have given me all that I have, all that I am, and I surrender all to your divine will. Give me only your love and your grace. With this I am rich enough, and I have no more to ask. In Jesus' name. Amen. *St. Ignatius of Loyola*

PSALM 55:16, 18, 22—But I call upon God, and the LORD will save me . . . He will redeem me unharmed from the battle I wage, for many are arrayed against me . . . Cast your burden on the LORD, and he will sustain you; he will never permit the righteous to be moved.

GENESIS 41:38-40a, 41 *I Have Set You Over Egypt*
Pharaoh said to his servants, "Can we find anyone else like this—one in whom is the spirit of God?" So Pharaoh said to Joseph, "Since God has shown you all this . . . you shall be over my house, and all my people shall order themselves as you command . . . See, I have set you over all the land of Egypt."

1 CORINTHIANS 4:5 *The Lord Will Disclose the Purposes of the Heart*
Therefore do not pronounce judgment . . . before the Lord comes, who will bring to light the things now hidden in darkness and will disclose the purposes of the heart. Then each one will receive commendation from God.

MARK 2:23—3:6 *Today's Gospel Reading*

Your continual prayer should be for faith and love. I admired a holy man in France who, considering the state of one who was full of doubts and fears, forbade him to think of his *sins* at all and ordered him to think only of the love of God in Christ. All his fears vanished away and he lived and died in the triumph of faith. JOHN WESLEY, *LETTER TO MARY BISHOP*, 1770

EVENING REFLECTIONS

PSALM 138:7-8b—Though I walk in the midst of trouble, you preserve me against the wrath of my enemies; you stretch out your hand, and your right hand delivers me. The LORD will fulfill his purpose for me; your steadfast love, O LORD, endures forever.

PRAYER—Merciful Father, accept my sincere thanks and praise for life and every other blessing of your grace. You have redeemed me by your blood and sanctified me by the grace of your Holy Spirit. For these and all other mercies, I praise and magnify your glorious name. Amen. *JW*

WEEK TWO
Lenten Season

Sunday: Lose Your Life to Save It

Read the Gospel passage from Mark 8:31-38 and the devotional reflection titled "Lose Your Life to Save It," then respond to the discussion prompts in the Reflective Journaling section.

THE MUSIC OF ASHES TO FIRE

Week 2: "My Savior's Love" (Track 3)

Monday through Saturday of Week 2

IN THE MORNING:

A personal daily devotional guide includes prayer, a reading from the Old Testament, the Psalms, the Epistles, and the Gospel for each day of the week.

This week's readings are from Genesis, 1 Corinthians, and the Gospel of Mark.

Inspirational quotes from men and women of faith keep us in contact with our shared Christian heritage.

IN THE EVENING:

An evening psalm and prayer become preludes to nighttime rest and renewal.

LENTEN SEASON–WEEK TWO
Lose Your Life to Save It

A devotional reflection based on Mark 8:31-38

Read the Gospel passage first, then the devotional reflection that follows. The discussion prompts at the end will help prepare you for Sunday school and small-group sessions.

Some things Jesus said are just plain hard to stomach. In fact, whole books have been written on the "hard sayings of Jesus." Just ask Peter, the apostle. He was feeling pretty good after Jesus commended him for recognizing his master as the Messiah (see Mark 8:29). But then the Lord began to talk about suffering, rejection, and being killed. So Peter, brimming with confidence, took Jesus aside and told him not to talk this way. As everyone knows, God would never let such things happen to his Messiah.

That's when it happened. Jesus turned to Peter in a holy rage and said, "Get behind me, Satan!" (v. 33). Peter had been called a lot of things in his life, but when his beloved Teacher called him Satan, it stunned Peter and the other disciples into bewildered silence. Jesus said Peter was seeing things only from a human point of view and not according to God's plan.

To fully understand Jesus' harsh words to Peter, we have to go back to the Lord's first recorded temptations in the wilderness. All the attacks of Satan can be reduced to one fundamental challenge Jesus faced all through his ministry: it was the temptation to reach for the crown without first enduring the cross. After all, Jesus was the Son of God, the second person of the Trinity! Why not call upon his status and power to demonstrate his Lordship and bring peace on earth?

But that was not the Father's plan. The Son was called to walk the path of suffering servanthood and pour out his life as an atoning sacrifice. This was what Peter and the other disciples could not understand. So when Peter confidently told Jesus he would never have to suffer, Jesus recognized a familiar voice—not the voice of Peter, but the sinister voice of his great adversary, once again enticing the Lord to avoid the cross. That's why he said, "Get out of my way, Satan!"

With those devastating words still hanging in the air, Jesus seized the opportunity to teach a lesson in discipleship. He wanted it to be clear that the way of the cross was not only for the Son of Man but also for every person who answers the call to follow Christ. He said, "If any want to become my followers, let them deny themselves and take up their cross and follow me" (v. 34).

This is the first mention of the cross in Mark's Gospel. The Jews were sickened by the sight of their fellow Jews being crucified on Roman crosses. No Roman citizen could be executed this way. It was only for slaves, pirates, and enemies of the empire. Because Jesus was accused of proclaiming a rival kingdom, he would be crucified as an enemy of Caesar. In a typical crucifixion, the condemned was forced to carry the crossbar to the place of execution. There the crosspiece was attached to the upright post and the victim was stripped naked and hung by ropes or nails. Death was from blood loss, asphyxiation, or other injuries inflicted by Roman soldiers. It was gruesome, cruel, and humiliating.

What did the crowd think when they heard Jesus say that his followers must carry crosses? It was a horrifying image that could only be associated with death. Did Jesus mean the Romans would crucify all his followers? No, he was saying something very different. He was talking about a *voluntary* taking up of one's cross. He was inviting people to make a conscious choice to exchange one kind of life for another, to give up the life of the world in exchange for the kingdom of God.

Sometimes we hear people talk about having a "cross to bear." It might be a cantankerous in-law, a boss who's impossible to please, or an arthritic knee that whines every time the weather changes. These kinds of burdens and annoyances make life a daily challenge and test our reserves of grace and patience. But they are not the crosses Jesus calls us to carry. The cross of discipleship is exactly the same for every follower of Christ: *it's the cross upon which each of us is crucified to our own self-centered life.* When we willingly die this death, we are liberated into the life of the kingdom.

And though this cross requires self-denial, Jesus shows us that, paradoxically, it is in our eternal best interests. We die to the world that is passing away and receive in exchange a life of joyful service in the kingdom that will never end. As *The Message* says, "Self-sacrifice is the way, my way, to saving yourself, your true self. What good would it do to get everything you want and lose you, the real you? What could you ever trade your soul for?" (vv. 36-37).

There's one more thing everyone knew about Roman crosses. Once the cross was placed on your shoulders and you were pointed down the road toward the place of crucifixion, you weren't coming back. There were no more appeals for mercy or last-minute reprieves from the governor. The path of cross bearing is a one-way road.

This is the call to discipleship with Jesus. The One who willingly accepted the cost of messiahship invites us to follow him in a new kind of life and never turn back to the service of self and the love of the world. As the old song says, "I have decided to follow Jesus . . . The world behind me, the cross before me. No turning back, no turning back." —RP

After reading the passage from Mark 8:31-38 and
the devotional reflection "Lose Your Life to Save It,"
you may also want to read the following
related passages:
Genesis 17:1-7, 15-16; Psalm 22:23-31; Romans 4:13-25

The discussion prompts that follow will help prepare you to participate in your Sunday school class or small-group study. Use your Reflective Journaling section to record any other insights that come to you as you read the Gospel lesson and the devotional reflection.

DISCUSSION PROMPT NO. 1: MARK 8

Why do you think Peter rebuked Jesus? What do you think Peter might have said that prompted Jesus' rebuke and the teaching in verses 34-38?

DISCUSSION PROMPT NO. 2: MARK 8

How do self-denial, taking up one's cross, and following Jesus express a divine mind-set rather than a human one?

DISCUSSION PROMPT NO. 3: MARK 8

How do people who want to save their life end up losing it by refusing to take up their cross?

DISCUSSION PROMPT NO. 4: MARK 8

What might cause someone to be ashamed of Jesus' words?

DISCUSSION PROMPT NO. 5: DEVOTIONAL REFLECTION

What are the implications for your discipleship in the writer's comment: "Once the cross was placed on your shoulders and you were pointed down the road toward the place of crucifixion, you weren't coming back"?

REFLECTIVE JOURNALING

_____

_____

_____

_____

_____

_____

_____

_____

_____

_____

_____

_____

_____

_____

_____

_____

_____

_____

_____

_____

_____

_____

_____

PSALM 57 ▪ GENESIS 41:46-57 ▪ 1 CORINTHIANS 4:8-21 ▪ MARK 3:7-19a

MORNING MEDITATIONS

PRAYER—O God, you are the giver of all good gifts and I desire to praise your name for all of your goodness to me. I thank you for sending your Son to die for my sins, for the means of grace, and for the hope of glory, through Jesus Christ. Amen. **JW**

PSALM 57:1—Be merciful to me, O God, be merciful to me, for in you my soul takes refuge; in the shadow of your wings I will take refuge, until the destroying storms pass by.

GENESIS 41:53-54 *There Was Bread*
The seven years of plenty that prevailed in the land of Egypt came to an end; and the seven years of famine began to come, just as Joseph had said. There was famine in every country, but throughout the land of Egypt there was bread.

1 CORINTHIANS 4:10-12 *Fools for the Sake of Christ*
We are fools for the sake of Christ, but you are wise in Christ. We are weak, but you are strong. You are held in honor, but we in disrepute. To the present hour we are hungry and thirsty, we are poorly clothed and beaten and homeless, and we grow weary from the work of our own hands.

MARK 3:7-19a *Today's Gospel Reading*

My son, hear my words, words most sweet, excelling all the learning of philosopher and the wise men of this world. My words are spirit and life and are not to be weighed by human standards . . . Write my words in your heart, and think diligently on them; for they will be very necessary in the time of temptation.   THOMAS À KEMPIS, *THE IMITATION OF CHRIST*

EVENING REFLECTIONS

PSALM 65:1, 5—Praise is due to you, O God, in Zion; and to you shall vows be performed . . . By awesome deeds you answer us with deliverance, O God of our salvation; you are the hope of all the ends of the earth and of the farthest seas.

PRAYER (PSALM 51:17, 7)—O Lord, "the sacrifice acceptable to [you] is a broken spirit; a broken and contrite heart, O God, you will not despise . . . Purge me with hyssop, and I shall be clean; wash me, and I shall be whiter than snow." Amen.

PSALM 62 ▪ GENESIS 42:1-17 ▪ 1 CORINTHIANS 5:1-8 ▪ MARK 3:19b-35

MORNING MEDITATIONS

PRAYER—Open our eyes to behold your presence and strengthen our hands to do your will, that the world may rejoice and give you praise. Blessed are you, Sovereign God of all, to you be praise and glory forever. Amen.

PSALM 62:1-2, 8—For God alone by soul waits in silence; from him comes my salvation. He alone is my rock and my salvation, my fortress; I shall never be shaken . . . Trust in him at all times, O people; pour out your heart before him; God is a refuge for us.

GENESIS 42:3-5 *Joseph's Brothers Went Down to Buy Grain*
So ten of Joseph's brothers went down to buy grain in Egypt. But Jacob did not send Joseph's brother Benjamin . . . Thus the sons of Israel were among the other people who came to buy grain, for the famine had reached the land of Canaan.

1 CORINTHIANS 5:7-8 *Our Paschal Lamb Has Been Sacrificed*
Clean out the old yeast so that you may be a new batch, as you really are unleavened. For our paschal lamb, Christ, has been sacrificed. Therefore, let us celebrate the festival, not with the old yeast, the yeast of malice . . . but with the unleavened bread of sincerity and truth.

MARK 3:19b-35 *Today's Gospel Reading*

Learn to know the dignity of your nature. Remember that image of God in which you were created, which, though defaced by Adam, is now restored in Christ . . . Let us listen to the Apostle's words, "For you have died and your life is hid with Christ in God. When Christ who is our life appears, then you also will appear with him in glory."

ST. LEO THE GREAT, *SERMON 7*

EVENING REFLECTIONS

PSALM 68:19-20a, 35b—Blessed be the Lord, who daily bears us up; God is our salvation. Our God is a God of salvation . . . he gives power and strength to his people.

PRAYER (PSALM 51:17, 10)—O Lord, "the sacrifice acceptable to [you] is a broken spirit; a broken and contrite heart, O God, you will not despise . . . Create in me a clean heart, O God, and put a new and right spirit within me." Amen.

PSALM 72 ▪ GENESIS 42:18-25 ▪ 1 CORINTHIANS 5:9—6:11 ▪ MARK 4:1-20

MORNING MEDITATIONS

PRAYER—Lord God, send your Holy Spirit to be the guide of all my ways and the sanctifier of my soul and body. Give me the light of your presence, your peace from heaven, and the salvation of my soul, through Jesus Christ my Lord. Amen. **JW**

PSALM 72:18-19—Blessed be the LORD, the God of Israel, who alone does wondrous things. Blessed be his glorious name forever; may his glory fill the whole earth. Amen and Amen.

GENESIS 42:21 *We Are Paying the Penalty*
Alas, we are paying the penalty for what we did to our brother; we saw his anguish when he pleaded with us, but we would not listen. That is why this anguish has come upon us.

1 CORINTHIANS 6:9a, 11 *You Were Justified in the Name of Jesus*
Do you not know that wrongdoers will not inherit the kingdom of God? . . . And this is what some of you used to be. But you were washed, you were sanctified, you were justified in the name of the Lord Jesus Christ and in the Spirit of our God.

MARK 4:1-20 *Today's Gospel Reading*

How precious is the gift of the cross . . . For it is a tree which brings forth life, not death. It is the source of light, not darkness. It offers you a home in Eden. It does not cast you out. It is the tree which Christ mounted, and so destroyed the devil, and rescued the human race from slavery to the tyrant.

ST. THEODORE THE STUDITE, *ON THE ADORATION OF THE CROSS*

EVENING REFLECTIONS

PSALM 119:89-90—The LORD exists forever; your word stands firmly fixed in heaven. Your faithfulness endures to all generations; you have established the earth, and it stands fast.

PRAYER (PSALM 51:17, 12)—O Lord, "the sacrifice acceptable to [you] is a broken spirit; a broken and contrite heart, O God, you will not despise . . . Restore to me the joy of your salvation, and sustain in me a willing spirit." Amen.

PSALM 70 ▪ GENESIS 42:26-38 ▪ 1 CORINTHIANS 6:12-20 ▪ MARK 4:21-34

MORNING MEDITATIONS

PRAYER—O Eternal God, my Savior and Lord, I acknowledge that all I am and all I have is yours. I pray that you will surround me with such a sense of your infinite goodness, that I may return to you all possible love and obedience, through Jesus Christ. Amen. *JW*

PSALM 70:4-5—Let all who seek you rejoice and be glad in you. Let those who love your salvation say evermore, "God is great!" But I am poor and needy; hasten to me, O God! You are my help and my deliverer; O LORD, do not delay!

GENESIS 42:26-28   *What Is This That God Has Done to Us?*
They loaded their donkeys with their grain . . . When one of them opened his sack . . . he saw his money at the top of the sack. He said to his brothers, "My money has been put back; here it is in my sack!" At this they lost heart and turned trembling to one another, saying, "What is this that God has done to us?"

1 CORINTHIANS 6:19-20   *Your Body Is a Temple*
Or do you not know that your body is a temple of the Holy Spirit within you, which you have from God, and that you are not your own? For you were bought with a price; therefore glorify God in your body.

MARK 4:21-34   *Today's Gospel Reading*

Just as the Father is seen in the Son, so the Son is seen in the Holy Spirit. Worship in the Spirit suggests the activity of our intelligence . . . Our Lord said that we must worship in Spirit and in truth, and by "truth" he clearly meant himself. We speak of worship in the Son, which is worship in the one who is the image of God the Father.

ST. BASIL THE GREAT, *ON THE HOLY SPIRIT*

EVENING REFLECTIONS

PSALM 74:12-13a, 15-16—Yet God my King is from of old, working salvation in the earth. You divided the sea by your might . . . You cut openings for springs and torrents; you dried up ever-flowing streams. Yours is the day, yours also the night; you established the luminaries and the sun.

PRAYER (PSALM 51:17, 6)—O Lord, "the sacrifice acceptable to [you] is a broken spirit; a broken and contrite heart, O God, you will not despise . . . You desire truth in the inward being; therefore teach me wisdom in my secret heart." Amen.

PSALM 69:16-36 ▪ **GENESIS 43:1-15** ▪ **1 CORINTHIANS 7:1-20** ▪ **MARK 4:35-41**

MORNING MEDITATIONS

PRAYER—Holy God, in your compassion and mercy, your light breaks forth in our darkness and your healing springs up for our deliverance. Sustain us with your bountiful Spirit as we rejoice in your saving help, in the name of Christ, I pray. Amen.

PSALM 69:30, 32, 34a—I will praise the name of God with a song; I will magnify him with thanksgiving . . . Let the oppressed see it and be glad; you who seek God, let your hearts revive . . . Let heaven and earth praise him.

GENESIS 43:11a, 12-13, 15   *God Grant You Mercy*
Then their father Israel said to them, ". . . Take double the money with you. Carry back with you the money that was returned in the top of your sacks . . . Take your brother also, and be on your way . . . may God Almighty grant you mercy before the man" . . . So the men . . . went on their way down to Egypt, and stood before Joseph.

1 CORINTHIANS 7:17, 20   *Lead the Life the Lord Has Assigned*
However that may be, let each of you lead the life that the Lord has assigned, to which God called you. This is my rule in all the churches . . . Let each of you remain in the condition in which you were called.

MARK 4:35-41   *Today's Gospel Reading*

To prepare us for [covenant] life, God himself spoke the words of the Decalogue to everyone. And so these words remain with us too. By his coming in the flesh God did not revoke them; he extended and augmented them . . . that [we] might know God as Father and love him with all our hearts.   ST. IRENAEUS, *AGAINST HERESIES*

EVENING REFLECTIONS

PSALM 73:25, 28—Whom have I in heaven but you? And there is nothing on earth that I desire other than you . . . For me it is good to be near God; I have made the Lord GOD my refuge, to tell of all your works.

PRAYER (PSALM 51:17, 11)—O Lord, "the sacrifice acceptable to [you] is a broken spirit; a broken and contrite heart, O God, you will not despise . . . Do not cast me away from your presence, and do not take your holy spirit from me." Amen.

PSALM 76 ▪ GENESIS 43:16-34 ▪ 1 CORINTHIANS 7:21-32 ▪ MARK 5:1-20

MORNING MEDITATIONS

PRAYER—Blessed are you, Sovereign God, ruler and judge of all, creator and protector of life. All things praise your name. Put your grace into my heart so that my praise can join all of creation to magnify your great and glorious name, through Christ my Lord, Amen. **JW**

PSALM 76:1, 4, 7a—In Judah God is known, his name is great in Israel . . . Glorious are you, more majestic than the everlasting mountains . . . You indeed are awesome! Who can stand before you?

GENESIS 43:23, 29, 30a, c   *Your God Put the Treasure in Your Sacks*
[Joseph] replied, "Rest assured, do not be afraid; your God and the God of your father must have put treasure in your sacks for you; I received your money" . . . Then he looked up and saw his brother Benjamin . . . With that, Joseph hurried out . . . into a private room and wept there.

1 CORINTHIANS 7:29a, 31   *Time Has Grown Short*
I mean, brothers and sisters, the appointed time has grown short . . . [Let] those who deal with the world [do so] as though they had no dealings with it. For the present form of this world is passing away.

MARK 5:1-20   *Today's Gospel Reading*

Because God is good and especially good to those who serve him, we must cling to him, and be with him with all our soul and with all our heart and with all our strength. This we must do if we are to live in his light.   ST. AMBROSE, *ON FLIGHT FROM THE WORLD*

EVENING REFLECTIONS

PSALM 23:1-3—The LORD is my shepherd, I shall not want. He makes me lie down in green pastures; he leads me beside still waters; he restores my soul. He leads me in right paths for his name's sake.

PRAYER (PSALM 51:17, 7)—O Lord, "the sacrifice acceptable to [you] is a broken spirit; a broken and contrite heart, O God, you will not despise . . . Purge me with hyssop, and I shall be clean; wash me, and I shall be whiter than snow." Amen.

WEEK THREE

LENTEN SEASON

Sunday: Whip of Cords

Read the Gospel passage from John 2:13-22 and the devotional reflection titled "Whip of Cords," then respond to the discussion prompts in the Reflective Journaling section.

THE MUSIC OF ASHES TO FIRE

Week 3: "Confluence" (Track 4)

Monday through Saturday of Week 3

IN THE MORNING:

A personal daily devotional guide includes prayer,
a reading from the Old Testament, the Psalms, the Epistles,
and the Gospel for each day of the week.

This week's readings are from Genesis,
1 Corinthians, and the Gospel of Mark.

Inspirational quotes from men and women of faith
keep us in contact with our shared Christian heritage.

IN THE EVENING:

An evening psalm and prayer become preludes
to nighttime rest and renewal.

LENTEN SEASON–WEEK THREE
Whip of Cords

A devotional reflection based on John 2:13-22

*R*ead the Gospel passage first, then the devotional reflection that follows. *The discussion prompts at the end will help prepare you for Sunday school and small-group sessions.*

For some reason, my mind's eye can see the John 2:13-22 event in the life of Christ more vividly than any other particular event recorded for us in the Gospel of John. Since childhood, this particular portion of John's narrative has captured my imagination. In fact, not only has my imagination been captured, but my life has been increasingly inspired as well.

In this passage, I imagine absolute bedlam. The money changers and merchandisers are groping for renegade coins on the muck-covered floor. I imagine the animals that had produced the muck scampering about. I imagine court officials, consumers, and onlookers pointing at Jesus and shouting their angry slurs at him in a frenzy of activity. I imagine Jesus firmly grasping and vigorously snapping a whip he hurriedly winds together in holy anger. I imagine Jesus increasingly raising his voice proportionally to the level of chaos. I imagine Jesus in full command of his humanity as he intentionally and with intensity contests such arrogance, insensitivity, and utter irreverence.

When I was a child, I found resonance with this specific passage because Jesus was portrayed to me in Sunday school to be something of the superhero I so badly wanted him to be. He went into a situation that *needed* to be turned upside down, and he did just that. Not only did he call out the nefarious ones, but like any good superhero he also advocated for the foreigners whose area of worship was taken up by the markets. Jesus stood up for those who couldn't stand up for themselves. (It is important to note that many scholars and Bible interpreters believe that the area in the temple the marketers were using to sell sacrifices and exchange money was called the Court of the Gentiles and was used for worship by non-Jewish people.)

When I was a teenager, I just found it easy to identify with a Jesus who got angry. Some of my frequent emotional outbursts and the outburst of Jesus might have been similar—even if he didn't sin in his anger and I may or may not have sinned in mine. As a teenager, this passage made Jesus understandable. It made Jesus accessible. It made Jesus real to me unlike any other passage. Jesus and I connected deeply through this story in John.

Now as an adult with dozens of years of spiritual experiences, scriptural readings, sermons, and prayers to speak into my knowledge and application of this passage, I not only "imagine" the story but am also inspired by it.

First, the depth of the humanity of Jesus inspires me. I find great assurance and encouragement because Jesus calls me to a life he understands. The Jesus we encounter in this passage is like us in many ways. He is human in every way, and he, too, has emotional outbursts of impatience and vexation. I am grateful that the life Jesus calls me to live is a life Jesus has already lived.

Second, the depth of Jesus' spirituality inspires me. In Jesus' anger he did not sin. This was, therefore, an instance of righteous indignation as opposed to an unholy fit of rage. This anger Jesus displayed was every bit as human as the anger we display. However, the anger of Jesus in this passage was held in equilibrium against his spirituality or his theology—a love for God his Father and a love for people.

Aside from the atonement acts leading to and executed on the cross and at the resurrection, there is no other passage in John (or in any of the other Gospels) that more clearly reveals the relationship between the humanity of Jesus and his own intentional pursuit of a life lived completely for God. I am inspired by Jesus' love for God and for others.

Third, I am inspired by the centrality of God's mission in the life of Jesus. Jesus very clearly states, "Stop making my Father's house a marketplace!" (v. 16). I contend that Jesus was angry that the foreigners were being pushed out. I also contend that he was even angrier that his Father's house was being used for purposes that did not bring glory to his Father. Jesus was always about his Father and the mission of his Father. His Father was central to his very being. Jesus was governed, not by opportunities to be angry for the sake of justice, but by a deep and acute love for his Father. Every kingdom act of Jesus was centered on his Father.

Fourth, the intentionality of Jesus to fulfill his mission inspires me. Jesus didn't just take on that particular year's Passover gathering of merchandisers. Jesus took on a system that was corrupt. This wasn't the first year the temple was being used for other purposes. Jesus, in his angry outburst, was taking on an entire system of wrongdoing. Not content with dealing merely with the symptoms of the problem (tables, coins, merchandisers, animals, etc.), Jesus got at the very root of the wrongdoing when he challenged the religious system. Judaism was so driven by its own set of laws that it was unable to imagine or interpret the divine message as found in Jesus. Jesus intentionally challenges the institution itself.

Finally, I am inspired by the totality in which Jesus viewed his life and calling. When the Jews, gathered in the temple court, challenged Jesus to produce a sign to prove his authority (v. 18), Jesus responds by saying, "Destroy this temple, and in three days I will raise it up" (v. 19). This response reveals that Jesus had in mind much more than the events on hand. The temple is Jesus. Jesus was proclaiming his death, burial, and resurrection. Jesus had in mind, in this display of holy anger and in every other event in the Gospels, that his life was not merely a life of calculated moments but a life characterized by a movement toward something greater—a new and whole life for all who believe.

Jesus' challenge to institutionalism is a great reminder to us all. Whether a challenge to the religious institutions of his day, or the current church of our day, each of us must be willing to ask the tough questions about the issues that permit the status quo to hinder revival. Institutions or religious practices don't reveal the presence of God, regardless of forms of worship or spiritual practice. The presence of God is mediated to a broken society in and through us—a body of people who, led by the Holy Spirit, choose to live, love, and lead in the way of Jesus.

Our goal during this Lenten season is to reflect not only on the purging of the temple as seen in John 2:13-22 but also on the purging of our own souls—for the sake of God's mission. —CF

After reading the passage from John 2:13-22 and the
devotional reflection "Whip of Cords," you may also
want to read the following related passages:
Exodus 20:1-17; Psalm 19; 1 Corinthians 1:18-25

The discussion prompts that follow will help prepare you to participate in your Sunday school class or small-group study. Use your Reflective Journaling section to record any other insights that come to you as you read the Gospel lesson and the devotional reflection.

DISCUSSION PROMPT NO. 1: JOHN 2

Why might Jesus want to have driven the money changers out of the temple?

DISCUSSION PROMPT NO. 2: JOHN 2

If you had been present for this event, what initial impression would you have formed of Jesus? Would this have been an accurate picture?

DISCUSSION PROMPT NO. 3: JOHN 2

Describe how Jesus' body was a temple. Why do you think he responded to the religious leaders the way he did?

DISCUSSION PROMPT NO. 4: DEVOTIONAL REFLECTION

The writer asserts that Jesus' anger was about more than social justice. What higher concerns motivated him?

DISCUSSION PROMPT NO. 5: JOHN 2

What practical implications might the purging of the temple have for twenty-first century believers?

REFLECTIVE JOURNALING

_____

_____

_____

_____

_____

_____

_____

_____

PSALM 80 ▪ GENESIS 44:18-34 ▪ 1 CORINTHIANS 8:1-6 ▪ MARK 5:21-43

MORNING MEDITATIONS

PRAYER (BCP)—Our Father in heaven, hallowed be your Name, your kingdom come, your will be done, on earth as it is in heaven. Give us today our daily bread. Forgive us our sins as we forgive those who sin against us. Save us from the time of trial, and deliver us from evil. For the kingdom, the power, and the glory are yours, now and for ever. Amen.

PSALM 80:7-8, 14a, 17—Restore us, O God of hosts; let your face shine, that we may be saved. You brought a vine out of Egypt; you drove out the nations and planted it . . . Turn again, O God of hosts . . . Let your hand be upon the one at your right hand, the one whom you made strong for yourself.

GENESIS 44:33-34 *Let the Boy Go Back*
Now therefore, please let your servant remain as a slave to my lord in place of the boy; and let the boy go back with his brothers. For how can I go back to my father if the boy is not with me? I fear to see the suffering that would come upon my father.

1 CORINTHIANS 8:6 *One Lord Jesus Christ*
Yet for us there is one God, the Father, from whom are all things and for whom we exist, and one Lord, Jesus Christ, through whom are all things and through whom we exist.

MARK 5:21-43 *Today's Gospel Reading*

The life that intends to be wholly obedient, wholly submissive, wholly listening, is astonishing in its completeness. Its joys are ravishing, its peace profound, its humility the deepest, its power world-shaking, its love enveloping, its simplicity that of a trusting child.
THOMAS R. KELLY, *A TESTAMENT OF DEVOTION*

EVENING REFLECTIONS

PSALM 79:8-9—Do not remember against us the iniquities of our ancestors; let your compassion come speedily to meet us . . . Help us, O God of our salvation, for the glory of your name; deliver us, and forgive our sins.

PRAYER—O God, let it be the one business of my life to glorify you by every thought of my heart, by every word of my tongue, by every work of my hand, and by professing your truth and love to everyone. Amen. *JW*

PSALM 78:1-39 ▪ GENESIS 45:1-15 ▪ 1 CORINTHIANS 8:7-13 ▪ MARK 6:1-13

MORNING MEDITATIONS

PRAYER (BCP)—Our Father in heaven, hallowed be your Name, **your kingdom come, your will be done, on earth as it is in heaven.** Give us today our daily bread. Forgive us our sins as we forgive those who sin against us. Save us from the time of trial, and deliver us from evil. For the kingdom, the power, and the glory are yours, now and for ever. Amen.

PSALM 78:1, 4—Give ear, O my people, to my teaching; incline your ears to the words of my mouth . . . we will tell to the coming generation the glorious deeds of the LORD, and his might, and the wonders that he has done.

GENESIS 45:1a, 2a, 3   *I Am Joseph*
Then Joseph . . . cried out, "Send everyone away from me." . . . And he wept so loudly that the Egyptians heard it . . . Joseph said to his brothers, "I am Joseph. Is my father still alive?" But his brothers could not answer him, so dismayed were they at his presence.

1 CORINTHIANS 8:12-13   *Do Not Wound the Conscience of the Weak*
But when you thus sin against members of your family, and wound their conscience when it is weak, you sin against Christ. Therefore, if food is a cause of their falling, I will never eat meat, so that I may not cause one of them to fall.

MARK 6:1-13   *Today's Gospel Reading*

The life of obedience is a holy life, a separated life, a renounced life, cut off from worldly compromises, distinct, heaven-dedicated in the midst of others, stainless as the snows upon the mountain tops.   THOMAS R. KELLY, *A TESTAMENT OF DEVOTION*

EVENING REFLECTIONS

PSALM 78:67a, 70-72—He rejected the tent of Joseph . . . He chose his servant David, and took him from the sheepfolds; from tending the nursing ewes he brought him to be the shepherd of his people Jacob . . . With upright heart he tended them, and guided them with skillful hand.

PRAYER—O Lamb of God, in this evening sacrifice of praise and prayer, I offer you a contrite heart. Give me grace, throughout my whole life, in every thought, and word, and work to imitate your meekness and humility, through Christ, my Lord, I pray. Amen. **JW**

PSALM 119:97-120 ▪ GENESIS 45:16-28 ▪ 1 CORINTHIANS 9:1-7 ▪
MARK 6:13-29

MORNING MEDITATIONS

PRAYER (BCP)—Our Father in heaven, hallowed be your Name, your kingdom come, your will be done, on earth as it is in heaven. **Give us today our daily bread.** Forgive us our sins as we forgive those who sin against us. Save us from the time of trial, and deliver us from evil. For the kingdom, the power, and the glory are yours, now and for ever. Amen.

PSALM 119:97-98, 105—Oh, how I love your law! It is my meditation all day long. Your commandment makes me wiser than my enemies, for it is always with me . . . Your word is a lamp to my feet and a light to my path.

GENESIS 45:25-26, 28 *My Son Joseph Is Alive*
So they went up out of Egypt and came to their father Jacob in the land of Canaan. And they told him, "Joseph is still alive! He is even ruler over all the land of Egypt." He was stunned; he could not believe them. But when they told him all the words of Joseph . . . Israel said, "Enough! My son Joseph is still alive. I must go and see him before I die."

1 CORINTHIANS 9:1b-3 *You Are the Seal of My Apostleship*
Are you not my work in the Lord? If I am not an apostle to others, at least I am to you; for you are the seal of my apostleship in the Lord. This is my defense to those who would examine me.

MARK 6:13-29 *Today's Gospel Reading*

Let inward prayer be your last act before you fall asleep and the first act when you awake. And in time you will find as did Brother Lawrence, that "those who have the gale of the Holy Spirit go forward even in sleep."   THOMAS R. KELLY, *A TESTAMENT OF DEVOTION*

EVENING REFLECTIONS

PSALM 82:3-4a, 8a—Give justice to the weak and the orphan; maintain the right of the lowly and the destitute. Rescue the weak and the needy . . . Rise up, O God, judge the earth.

PRAYER—O Lord, whose whole life cried out, "Father, not my will, but your will be done," give me grace to walk after your pattern and to follow in your steps. Give me grace to take up my cross, in Jesus name. **JW**

PSALM 43 ▪ GENESIS 46:1-7, 28-34 ▪ 1 CORINTHIANS 9:8-15 ▪ MARK 6:30-46

MORNING MEDITATIONS

PRAYER (BCP)—Our Father in heaven, hallowed be your Name, your kingdom come, your will be done, on earth as it is in heaven. Give us today our daily bread. **Forgive us our sins as we forgive those who sin against us.** Save us from the time of trial, and deliver us from evil. For the kingdom, the power, and the glory are yours, now and for ever. Amen.

PSALM 43:3-4—O send out your light and your truth; let them lead me; let them bring me to your holy hill and to your dwelling. Then I will go to the altar of God, to God my exceeding joy; and I will praise you . . . O God, my God.

GENESIS 46:1a, 2-3 *I Will Make of You a Great Nation*
When Israel set out on his journey with all that he had and came to Beer-sheba . . . God spoke to Israel in visions of the night, and said, "Jacob, Jacob." And he said, "Here I am." Then he said, "I am God, the God of your father; do not be afraid to go down to Egypt, for I will make of you a great nation there."

1 CORINTHIANS 9:10b, 14 *A Share in the Crop*
It was indeed written for our sake, for whoever plows should plow in hope and whoever threshes should thresh in hope of a share in the crop . . . In the same way, the Lord commanded that those who proclaim the gospel should get their living by the gospel.

MARK 6:30-46 *Today's Gospel Reading*

He who walks in obedience . . . living the life of inner prayer, of submission and exultation, on him God's holiness takes hold as a mastering passion of life . . . Humility and holiness are twins in the astonishing birth of obedience in the hearts of people.

THOMAS R. KELLY, *A TESTAMENT OF DEVOTION*

EVENING REFLECTIONS

PSALM 86:4-5—Gladden the soul of your servant, for to you, O Lord, I lift up my soul. For you, O Lord, are good and forgiving, abounding in steadfast love to all who call on you.

PRAYER—My Lord and my God, you see my heart; and my desires are not hidden from you. I am encouraged and strengthened by your goodness to me today. I want to be yours and yours alone. O my God, my Savior, my Sanctifier, hear me, help me, and show mercy to me for Jesus Christ's sake. Amen. *JW*

$\mathcal{F}$RIDAY

PSALM 88 ▪ GENESIS 47:1-26 ▪ 1 CORINTHIANS 9:16-27 ▪ MARK 6:47-56

MORNING MEDITATIONS

PRAYER (BCP)—Our Father in heaven, hallowed be your Name, your kingdom come, your will be done, on earth as it is in heaven. Give us today our daily bread. Forgive us our sins as we forgive those who sin against us. **Save us from the time of trial, and deliver us from evil.** For the kingdom, the power, and the glory are yours, now and for ever. Amen.

PSALM 88:13, 9b—But I, O LORD, cry out to you; in the morning my prayer comes before you. . . . Every day I call on you, O LORD; I spread out my hands to you.

GENESIS 47:4a, 4c, 6a-b   *The Land of Egypt Is Before You*
They said to Pharaoh, "We have come to reside as aliens in the land . . . Now, we ask you, let your servants settle in the land of Goshen." Then Pharaoh said to Joseph, ". . . The land of Egypt is before you; settle your father and your brothers in the best part of the land; let them live in the land of Goshen."

1 CORINTHIANS 9:19b, 22b-23   *All Things to All People*
I have made myself a slave to all, so that I might win more of them . . . I have become all things to all people, that I might by all means save some. I do it all for the sake of the gospel, so that I may share in its blessings.

MARK 6:47-56   *Today's Gospel Reading*

If you are willing to listen to me, then, servants of Christ, his brothers and co-heirs, I say that we should visit Christ while there is opportunity, take care of him and feed him. We should clothe Christ and welcome him.   GREGORY NAZIANZEN

EVENING REFLECTIONS

PSALM 92:1-2, 4a—It is good to give thanks to the LORD, to sing praises to your name, O Most High; to declare your steadfast love in the morning, and your faithfulness by night . . . for you, O LORD, have made me glad by your work.

PRAYER—Father, accept my imperfect repentance, have compassion on my infirmities, forgive my faults, purify my uncleanness, strengthen my weakness, fix my unstableness, and let your good Spirit watch over me forever, and your love ever rule in my heart, through the merits and sufferings and love of your Son, in whom you are always well pleased. Amen. **JW**

PSALM 87 ▪ GENESIS 47:27—48:7 ▪ 1 CORINTHIANS 10:1-13 ▪ MARK 7:1-12

MORNING MEDITATIONS

PRAYER (BCP)—Our Father in heaven, hallowed be your Name, your kingdom come, your will be done, on earth as it is in heaven. Give us today our daily bread. Forgive us our sins as we forgive those who sin against us. Save us from the time of trial, and deliver us from evil. **For the kingdom, the power, and the glory are yours, now and for ever. Amen.**

PSALM 87:1-3—On the holy mount stands the city he founded; the LORD loves the gates of Zion more than all the dwellings of Jacob. Glorious things are spoken of you, O city of God.

GENESIS 47:27, 29a, 30 *Carry Me Out of Egypt*
Thus Israel settled in the land of Egypt, in the region of Goshen; and they gained possessions in it, and were fruitful and multiplied exceedingly . . . When the time of Israel's death drew near, he called his son Joseph and said to him, ". . . When I lie down with my ancestors, carry me out of Egypt and bury me in their burial place." [Joseph] answered, "I will do as you have said."

1 CORINTHIANS 10:1b-4 *The Rock Was Christ*
Our ancestors were all under the cloud, and all passed through the sea, and all were baptized into Moses in the cloud and in the sea, and all ate the same spiritual food, and all drank the same spiritual drink. For they drank from the spiritual rock that followed them, and the rock was Christ.

MARK 7:1-12 *Today's Gospel Reading*

Run though all the words of the holy prayers [in Scripture], and I do not think that you will find anything in them that is not contained and included in the Lord's Prayer.

ST. AUGUSTINE, *LETTERS*

EVENING REFLECTIONS

PSALM 136:1, 11a, 12—O give thanks to the LORD, for he is good, for his steadfast love endures forever . . . [who] brought Israel out from [Egypt] . . . with a strong hand and an outstretched arm, for his steadfast love endures forever.

PRAYER—All the powers of my soul are too few to compose the thankful praise that is due to you. Yet you have declared that you will accept the sacrifice of thanksgiving, in return for all your goodness. Therefore, I will bless you, adore your power, and magnify your holy Name. Amen. *JW*

WEEK FOUR
Lenten Season

Sunday: Snake on a Pole

Read the Gospel passage from John 3:14-21 and the devotional reflection titled "Snake on a Pole," then respond to the discussion prompts in the Reflective Journaling section.

THE MUSIC OF ASHES TO FIRE

Week 4: "Come, Thou Fount of Every Blessing" (Track 5)

Monday through Saturday of Week 4

IN THE MORNING:

A personal daily devotional guide includes prayer, a reading from the Old Testament, the Psalms, the Epistles, and the Gospel for each day of the week.

This week's readings are from Exodus, 1 Corinthians, and the Gospel of Mark.

Inspirational quotes from men and women of faith keep us in contact with our shared Christian heritage.

IN THE EVENING:

An evening psalm and prayer become preludes to nighttime rest and renewal.

LENTEN SEASON–WEEK FOUR
Snake on a Pole

A devotional reflection based on John 3:14-21

*R*ead the Gospel passage first, then the devotional reflection that follows. The discussion prompts at the end will help prepare you for Sunday school and small-group sessions.

Nicodemus's mind was already reeling. Before he could even ask the important question, this rabbi was challenging everything he thought he knew. Born again? Born from above? It didn't make sense.

Then Jesus went on: "And as Moses lifted up the serpent in the wilderness, even so must the Son of Man be lifted up, that whoever believes in Him should not perish but have eternal life" (John 3:14-15, NKJV).

Nicodemus knew that story by heart. The Israelites had stumbled their way into the desert, murmuring and complaining all the way. What had started out as a freedom march had become a question of survival. Faith and obedience had deteriorated into sinful complaining against God and against God's man Moses. The writhing mass of fierce fiery snakes that began to attack them set them to crying for mercy. And mercy came in the promise that if they would look to the bronze serpent Moses raised on a pole, they would survive the snake bite and live. It was simply "Look—*and live!*"

What in the world did a snake on a pole have to do with being born again? Could a person be lifted up like the snake on a pole? The thoughts came too fast to compute.

But there was more. For just then Jesus took all the love of God, all the wisdom and treasure of heaven, and all the hopes and longing of humankind and said them in a single sentence, to one man, a Pharisee and ruler of the Jews. He said: "For God so loved the world that He gave His only begotten Son, that whoever believes in Him should not perish but have everlasting life" (v. 16, NKJV).

Nicodemus was a Pharisee; he knew the rules. But Jesus was talking about eternal life as a gift! A gift! Look and live? Isn't God the Judge of humankind, holding us accountable when we break the rules?

His thoughts raced as he heard Jesus go on: "For God did not send His Son into the world to condemn the world, but that the world through Him might be saved" (v. 17, NKJV). It began to dawn on Nicodemus that God's love might be greater, much greater than he had ever imagined. It might be harder to be damned than he had previously thought—or, at least, much simpler to be saved!

This week's message is not simplistic, but it is deceptively simple. There is life in a look! How simple is that? We know these verses well—but like Nicodemus, maybe we need to hear them again for the first time. Jesus is going to be lifted up where everyone can see him; those who look to him for life will receive life. Jesus was telling Nicodemus there is life for a look at the Man lifted up from the earth. There is an answer for every cry to God that asks for help!

Psalm 107 can shed some light on the simplicity of what Jesus was trying to express to Nicodemus. Four times in that beautiful psalm there is a story of people in desperate trouble. Not snakes in a wilderness, but real trouble, life-threatening trouble. Whether from ignorance, or rebellion, downright foolishness, or even merely pagan godlessness, this psalm pictures how people apart from God and grace finally come to realize they are at a dead end.

Our lesson today focuses on verses 17-19: "Fools, because of their transgression, and because of their iniquities, were afflicted . . . and they drew near to the gates of death. Then they cried out to the LORD in their trouble, and He saved them out of their distresses" (NKJV). They simply cried out and the Lord saved them. Salvation for a cry! Life for a look!

Being born again, born from above, is a holy mystery. Some things are actually too holy to try to "explain" even though they are smashingly real! Can being saved actually be as simple as what Jesus tried to tell Nicodemus the Pharisee? It is exactly that simple. We can look to the Son of Man, and we can be saved!

God responds to a look. He answers the faintest cry for help. Wherever we are on our spiritual journey, deeply concerned for our sin, just reaching out for faith to believe, or in the ongoing struggles of life, God is there.

There is an ancient prayer that can distill in twelve words the utter simplicity of our salvation. It is called the Jesus Prayer. Pray it often: "Lord Jesus Christ, Son of God, have mercy on me, a sinner." —RFM

***After reading the passage from John 3:14-21 and the
devotional reflection "Snake on a Pole," you may also
want to read the following related passages:***

Numbers 21:4-9; Psalm 107:1-3, 17-22; Ephesians 2:1-10

The discussion prompts that follow will help prepare you to participate in your Sunday school class or small-group study. Use your Reflective Journaling section to record any other insights that come to you as you read the Gospel lesson and the devotional reflection.

DISCUSSION PROMPT NO. 1: JOHN 3

Read Numbers 21:4-9. What similarities do you see between the story of the bronze serpent and Jesus' ministry?

DISCUSSION PROMPT NO. 2: JOHN 3

While some people are condemned for their unbelief, Jesus indicates that his primary purpose for coming into the world is salvation. How does this knowledge shape our view of God? Of condemnation?

DISCUSSION PROMPT NO. 3: JOHN 3

John 3:19 says that "light has come into the world." What does this mean?

DISCUSSION PROMPT NO. 4: JOHN 3

What is the connection between unbelief and the judgment described in verses 19-21?

DISCUSSION PROMPT NO. 5: DEVOTIONAL REFLECTION

Read 2 Kings 18:1-8. What happened to the bronze serpent? What warnings does this passage have for us today?

REFLECTIVE JOURNALING

_____

_____

_____

_____

_____

PSALM 89:1-18 ▪ **GENESIS 49:1-28** ▪ **1 CORINTHIANS 10:14—11:1** ▪ **MARK 7:24-37**

MORNING MEDITATIONS

PRAYER—For Your mercies' sake, O Lord my God, tell me what you are to me. Say to my soul: "I am your salvation." So speak that I may hear, O Lord; my heart is listening; open it that it may hear you, and say to my soul: "I am your salvation." After hearing this word, may I come to you in haste. *St. Augustine*

PSALM 89:1, 13-14—I will sing of your steadfast love, O LORD, forever; . . . You have a mighty arm; strong is your hand . . . Righteousness and justice are the foundation of your throne; steadfast love and faithfulness go before you.

GENESIS 49:22a, 24b-25a, 26a, c *The Last Words of Jacob*
Joseph is a fruitful bough . . . [and] by the hands of the Mighty One of Jacob, by the name of the Shepherd, the Rock of Israel, by the God of your father, who will help you, by the Almighty who will bless you with blessings of heaven above . . . [may] the blessings of your father . . . be on the head of Joseph.

1 CORINTHIANS 10:31—11:1 *Do Everything for the Glory of God*
So, whether you eat or drink, or whatever you do, do everything for the glory of God. Give no offense to Jews or to Greeks or to the church of God, just as I try to please everyone in everything I do, not seeking my own advantage, but that of many, so that they may be saved. Be imitators of me, as I am of Christ.

MARK 7:24-37 *Today's Gospel Reading*

The Church asserts that there is a Mind which made the universe, that he made it because he is the sort of Mind that takes pleasure in creation, and that if we want to know what the Mind of the Creator is, we must look at Christ. DOROTHY SAYERS, *CREED OR CHAOS?*

EVENING REFLECTIONS

PSALM 89:5-6, 8—Let the heavens praise your wonders, O LORD, your faithfulness in the assembly of the holy ones. For who in the skies can be compared to the LORD? . . . who is as mighty as you, O LORD? Your faithfulness surrounds you.

PRAYER—Lord, make me an instrument of Thy peace. Where there is hatred, let me sow love, where there is injury, pardon; where there is doubt, faith; where there is despair, hope. Amen. *Attributed to St. Francis of Assisi*

PSALM 99 ▪ GENESIS 49:29—50:14 ▪ 1 CORINTHIANS 11:17-34 ▪ MARK 8:1-10

MORNING MEDITATIONS

PRAYER—Lord, . . . [l]et me see your face even if I die, lest I die with longing to see it. The house of my soul is too small to receive you; let it be enlarged by you. It is all in ruins; I ask you to repair it. There are things in it, I confess and know, that must offend you. From my secret sins cleanse me, O Lord, and from all others spare your servant. Amen. **St. Augustine**

PSALM 99:1-2a, 4—The Lord is king: let the people tremble! He sits enthroned upon the cherubim; let the earth quake! The Lord is great in Zion . . . Mighty King, lover of justice . . . you have executed justice and righteousness in Jacob.

GENESIS 49:29, 31, 33 *Bury Me with My Ancestors*
"I am about to be gathered to my people. Bury me with my ancestors—in the cave in the field of Ephron . . . There Abraham and his wife Sarah were buried; there Isaac and his wife Rebekah were buried; and there I buried Leah" . . . When Jacob ended his charge to his sons, he . . . breathed his last.

1 CORINTHIANS 11:23b, 24-26 *Until He Comes*
The Lord Jesus . . . took a loaf of bread, and when he had given thanks, he broke it and said, "This is my body that is for you. Do this in remembrance of me" . . . He took the cup also . . . saying, "This cup is the new covenant in my blood. Do this . . . in remembrance of me." For as often as you eat this bread and drink this cup, you proclaim the Lord's death until he comes.

MARK 8:1-10 *Today's Gospel Reading*

We shall discover a Mind that loved his own creation so completely that he became part of it, suffered with it and for it, and made it a sharer in his own glory and a fellow worker with himself in the working out of his own design for it.   DOROTHY SAYERS, *CREED OR CHAOS?*

EVENING REFLECTIONS

PSALM 94:12, 13a, 18, 19b—Happy are those whom you discipline, O Lord, and whom you teach out of your law . . . When I thought, "My foot is slipping," your steadfast love, O Lord, held me up . . . your consolations cheered my soul.

PRAYER—Lord, make me an instrument of Thy peace. Where there is hatred, let me sow love . . . Where there is darkness, light; where there is sadness, joy. Amen. **Attributed to St. Francis of Assisi**

PSALM 109:1-4, 20-30 ▪ GENESIS 50:15-26 ▪ 1 CORINTHIANS 12:1-11 ▪ MARK 8:11-26

MORNING MEDITATIONS

PRAYER—O Lord my God, teach my heart where and how to seek you, where and how to find you. Lord, if you are not here but absent, where shall I seek you? But you are everywhere, so you must be here, therefore let me seek you. Amen. *St. Anselm of Canterbury*

PSALM 109:21, 26-27—But you, O Lord my Lord, act on my behalf for your name's sake; because your steadfast love is good, deliver me . . . Save me according to your steadfast love. Let them know that this is your hand; you, O Lord, have done it.

GENESIS 50:19-20   *God Intended It for Good*
Joseph said to them, "Do not be afraid! Am I in the place of God? Even though you intended to do harm to me, God intended it for good, in order to preserve a numerous people."

1 CORINTHIANS 12:4-6, 11   *By the Same Spirit*
Now there are varieties of gifts, but the same Spirit; and there are varieties of services, but the same Lord; and there are varieties of activities, but it is the same God who activates all of them in everyone . . . by one and the same Spirit, who allots to each one individually just as the Spirit chooses.

MARK 8:11-26   *Today's Gospel Reading*

Christ was seldom very encouraging to those who demanded signs, or lightning from heaven, and God is too subtle and too economical a craftsman to make very much use of those methods. But he takes our sins and errors and turns them into victories, as he made the crime of the Crucifixion to be the salvation of the world.

DOROTHY SAYERS, *CREED OR CHAOS?*

EVENING REFLECTIONS

PSALM 119:124-125, 135—Deal with your servant according to your steadfast love, and teach me your statutes. I am your servant; give me understanding, so that I may know your decrees . . . Make your face shine upon your servant, and teach me your statutes.

PRAYER—Lord, make me an instrument of Thy peace; where there is hatred, let me sow love . . . O Divine Master, grant that I may not so much seek to be consoled as to console, to be understood, as to understand, to be loved, as to love. Amen. ***Attributed to St. Francis of Assisi***

PSALM 69:31-38 ▪ EXODUS 1:6-22 ▪ 1 CORINTHIANS 12:12-26 ▪ MARK 8:27—9:1

MORNING MEDITATIONS

PRAYER—Lord, I am not trying to make my way to your height, for my understanding is in no way equal to that, but I do desire to understand a little of your truth which my heart already believes and loves. I do not seek to understand so that I may believe, but I believe so that I may understand; and what is more, I believe that unless I do believe I shall not understand. *St. Anselm of Canterbury*

PSALM 69:30-31a, 32, 35a—I will praise the name of God with a song; I will magnify him with thanksgiving. This will please the LORD . . . Let the oppressed see it and be glad; you who seek God, let your hearts revive . . . for God will save Zion.

EXODUS 1:8, 22   *A King Arose Who Did Not Know Joseph*
Now a new king arose over Egypt, who did not know Joseph . . . Then Pharaoh commanded all his people, "Every boy that is born to the Hebrews you shall throw into the Nile, but you shall let every girl live."

1 CORINTHIANS 12:12-13   *Baptized into One Body*
For just as the body is one and has many members, and all the members of the body, though many, are one body, so it is with Christ. For in the one Spirit we were all baptized into one body—Jews or Greeks, slaves or free—and we were all made to drink of one Spirit.

MARK 8:27—9:1   *Today's Gospel Reading*

When Judas sinned, Jesus paid; he brought good out of evil, he led out in triumph from the gates of Hell and brought all mankind out with him; but the suffering of Jesus and the sin of Judas remain a reality. God did not abolish the fact of evil: he transformed it. He did not stop the Crucifixion; he rose from the dead.   DOROTHY SAYERS, *CREED OR CHAOS?*

EVENING REFLECTIONS

PSALM 73:25-26—Whom have I in heaven but you? And there is nothing on earth that I desire other than you. My flesh and my heart may fail, but God is the strength of my heart and my portion forever.

PRAYER—Lord, make me an instrument of Thy peace; where there is hatred, let me sow love . . . For it is in giving, that we receive, it is in pardoning, that we are pardoned, it is in dying, that we are born to eternal life. *Attributed to St. Francis of Assisi*

PSALM 102 ▪ EXODUS 2:1-25 ▪ 1 CORINTHIANS 12:27—13:3 ▪ MARK 9:2-13

MORNING MEDITATIONS

PRAYER—O God, the author of peace and lover of concord, to know you is eternal life, to serve you is perfect freedom: defend us your servants from all assaults of our enemies, that we may trust in your defense and not fear the power of any adversaries; through Jesus Christ our Lord. Amen.

PSALM 102:18-19a, 20-21a—Let this be recorded for a generation to come, so that a people yet unborn may praise the LORD; that he looked down from his holy height . . . to hear the groans of the prisoners, to set free those who were doomed to die; so that the name of the LORD may be declared in Zion.

EXODUS 2:23b-25 *God Heard Their Groaning*
The Israelites groaned under their slavery, and cried out. Out of the slavery their cry for help rose up to God. God heard their groaning, and God remembered his covenant with Abraham, Isaac, and Jacob. God looked upon the Israelites, and God took notice of them.

1 CORINTHIANS 12:28, 31a *Strive for the Greater Gifts*
God has appointed in the church first apostles, second prophets, third teachers; then deeds of power, then gifts of healing, forms of assistance, forms of leadership, various kinds of tongues . . . Strive for the greater gifts.

MARK 9:2-13 *Today's Gospel Reading*

Now indeed the [disciples] could go out and "do something" about the problem of sin and suffering. They had seen the strong hands of God twist the crown of thorns into a crown of glory and in hands as strong as that they knew themselves safe.

DOROTHY SAYERS, *CREED OR CHAOS?*

EVENING REFLECTIONS

PSALM 107:10, 12a, 13-14—Some sat in darkness and in gloom, prisoners in misery and in irons . . . Then they cried to the LORD in their trouble, and he saved them . . . he brought them out of darkness and gloom, and broke their bonds asunder.

PRAYER—Father, strengthen the hearts of your church and all your servants. Give us grace to consecrate ourselves faithfully and entirely to your service. Help us to encourage one another in love and grow together as your people, through the merits of our Lord and Savior Jesus Christ. Amen. *JW*

PSALM 108:1-13 ▪ EXODUS 2:23-3:15 ▪ 1 CORINTHIANS 13:1-13 ▪ MARK 9:14-29

MORNING MEDITATIONS

PRAYER—God be in my head, and in my understanding; God be in mine eyes, and in my looking; God be in my mouth, and in my speaking; God be in my heart, and in my thinking; God be at mine end, and at my departing. Through Christ, my Lord, I pray. Amen. *Celtic prayer*

PSALM 108:1c-3—Awake, my soul! Awake, O harp and lyre! I will awake the dawn. I will give thanks to you, O LORD, among the peoples, and I will sing praises to you among the nations.

EXODUS 3:11-12   *I Will Be with You*
Moses said to God, "Who am I that I should go to Pharaoh, and bring the Israelites out of Egypt?" He said, "I will be with you; and this shall be the sign for you . . . when you have brought the people out of Egypt, you shall worship God on this mountain."

1 CORINTHIANS 13:12-13   *Then I Will Know*
Now we see in a mirror, dimly, but then we will see face to face. Now I know only in part; then I will know fully, even as I have been fully known. And now faith, hope, and love abide, these three; and the greatest of these is love.

MARK 9:14-29   *Today's Gospel Reading*

They had expected an earthly Messiah, and they beheld the Soul of Eternity. It had been said to them of old time, "No man shall look upon my face and live"; but for them a means had been found. They had seen the face of the living God turned upon them; and it was the face of a suffering and rejoicing Man.   DOROTHY SAYERS, *CREED OR CHAOS?*

EVENING REFLECTIONS

PSALM 33:18-21—Truly the eye of the LORD is on those . . . who hope in his steadfast love, to deliver their soul from death . . . Our soul waits for the LORD; he is our help and shield. Our heart is glad in him, because we trust in his holy name.

PRAYER—Father, you have promised to accept my thanksgiving and praise as an expression of my gratitude for your goodness. I will always bless your name, adore your power and magnify your grace. Help me to sing of your righteousness and proclaim your salvation day after day. Amen. *JW*

WEEK FIVE

LENTEN SEASON

Sunday: A Single Seed

Read the Gospel passage from John 12:20-33 and the
devotional reflection titled "A Single Seed," then respond to the
discussion prompts in the Reflective Journaling section.

THE MUSIC OF ASHES TO FIRE

Week 5: "Rhythm of Grace" (Track 6)

Monday through Saturday of Week 5

IN THE MORNING:

A personal daily devotional guide includes prayer,
a reading from the Old Testament, the Psalms, the Epistles,
and the Gospel for each day of the week.

This week's readings are from Exodus,
1 and 2 Corinthians, and the Gospel of Mark.

Inspirational quotes from men and women of faith
keep us in contact with our shared Christian heritage.

IN THE EVENING:

An evening psalm and prayer become preludes
to nighttime rest and renewal.

LENTEN SEASON–WEEK FIVE
A Single Seed

A devotional reflection based on John 12:20-33

*R*ead the Gospel passage first, then the devotional reflection that follows. The discussion prompts at the end will help prepare you for Sunday school and small-group sessions.

The inns in Jerusalem were filled with visitors from the surrounding area. There was a festive atmosphere among the crowd that came to celebrate the Feast of the Passover, not quite as festive as a New Orleans Mardi Gras, but people meeting and greeting friends as they jostled in the markets and streets. There was a heightened air of anticipation that energized the crowd after the unscheduled parade of palm waving for the newest celebrity in town. And celebrity is what they followed and wanted; the curious wanted to see this Jesus.

There were some visitors, identified as Greeks, who recognized a man named Philip whom they may have encountered earlier in a market. That encounter led them to believe he knew this celebrity Jesus. They stopped Philip and asked if he could arrange an interview with his Friend, or at least a sighting. Philip had to go through channels and found and told Andrew about the request. Together, Philip and Andrew arranged a meeting with Jesus. What an interview it became!

Their anticipation of such a thrill on meeting this "celebrity," who had engendered such excitement in the palm parade, left them puzzled when he began to speak to them. Imagine a ticker tape parade in New York City for a presidential candidate, or even for a series-winning sports team, headed for Disney World. Would such a person or sports star address the crowd with sobering comments? What was Jesus saying to them: "What are you expecting of me? You may be seeking to bask in my celebrity status. You *will* see my glorification, but not in the way you expect!"

Was this the same man who rode in triumph on a donkey in the parade? Why does he start by telling them he was like a single seed, or kernel of wheat, useless, unless planted and transformed in soil to produce more life, more seeds? What is he talking about? Seeds? Farming? He didn't talk to them about his accomplishments, or his miracles, as they expected such a hero to do. He was talking in riddles, metaphors, like so many of the parables he taught. He did not reference his earthly life but talked about his coming purpose. He hoped they would later understand that he would have to be "planted" in order to bring about many seeds.

The crowd, and we, have to think about this concept carefully. It is so foreign to our understanding. They had been eager to see this hero who had been heralded with hosannas, and they wanted to get close to his popularity, but he was saying that loss of life is good and love of life is loss. Hadn't they traveled to Jerusalem to celebrate the great feast of their faith, the Passover, when God miraculously saved their ancestors from slavery and loss of life in Egypt? God delivered the Israelites from destruction, but Jesus now says that losing one's life is better. This is not what they wanted to hear. They wanted Sunday's party atmosphere to continue. Losing one's life is a hard concept for us, too, when many of our magazines and television documentaries and advertisements bombard us with the importance of pursuing pleasure in this life, defying aging, and cheating death. Jesus sobers us with the foreign idea of losing our lives for the greater good.

While the audience is puzzling over how it can be good to lose one's life, Jesus talks about a new covenant with his people. "Did he mean Passover is changing?" they may have thought. "We've always been taught about our fathers' traditions and faithfully observe them." "Our Torah? How can we grasp this *new* covenant? Innermost being? Seeds that sprout from deep within?" The people must have been perplexed.

But Jesus talks about a new covenant, one that will be revealed in hearts and minds, deep within one's inner life (Jer. 31:33). A new covenant, radically different from their tradition, would lead to sacrifice and service to Christ as *the way* of bringing honor to the Father. As Jesus responded to the crowd, he cautioned them that if they were seeking to follow a popular leader, they would be disappointed. They would have to follow him, not *for* his popularity, but *in* his suffering. And this new covenant, not of laws and sacrifices, but of losing one's life to service would lead to eternal salvation *through* Jesus' sufferings. This was the glory (see Heb. 5:8-9) Jesus looked forward to, a new Passover of death.

Was the crowd disillusioned that this acclaimed hero was troubled and saddened by his popularity? Probably so. In their hearing, Jesus affirmed to the Father that he would not seek an escape from the plan of salvation. He was to face death as a single seed of grain in order to bring forth eternal life for all. "Should I say—'Father, save me from this hour'? No, it is for this reason that I have come to this hour. Father, glorify your name" (John 12:27-28a).

Out of heaven came a response to Jesus' resolve. The crowd must have looked at each other in bewilderment, "What was that?" Some thought the voice was thunder; others thought it was an angel who spoke to Jesus. Jesus assured them that the voice was a witness to the crowd, not to Jesus who was soon to face his death. The crowd that day became witnesses to Jesus' coming glorification.

There was a lot to talk about. They had a Passover to remember. Old things were passing away; all things were becoming new. The Seed—a single grain of wheat, the Son of God—would have to die for our sin and be buried until the third day, when he would be transformed in resurrection triumph. That buried seed produced seeds of redemption that have been sown throughout the ages and throughout the world. They grow in you and me, in our hearts and deep within our inner lives, yielding a harvest—eternal salvation. —HM

After reading the passage from John 12:20-33 and the devotional reflection "A Single Seed," you may also want to read the following related passages:
Jeremiah 31:31-34; Psalm 51:1-12; and Hebrews 5:5-10

The discussion prompts that follow will help prepare you to participate in your Sunday school class or small-group study. Use your Reflective Journaling section to record any other insights that come to you as you read the Gospel lesson and the devotional reflection.

DISCUSSION PROMPT NO. 1: JOHN 12
Explain what Jesus was trying to communicate about his death in verses 22-24?

DISCUSSION PROMPT NO. 2: JOHN 12
Why does the person who loves his or her life lose it, while the one who hates his or her life will keep it for eternity?

DISCUSSION PROMPT NO. 3: JOHN 12

God the Father spoke to Jesus before the crowd in an audible way. How does God speak to us today?

DISCUSSION PROMPT NO. 4: JOHN 12

How does lifting up Christ draw people to him? How does this glorify him?

DISCUSSION PROMPT NO. 5: DEVOTIONAL REFLECTION

How does the writer understand the analogy of the single seed of grain that dies? What does that have to say about your own spiritual life?

REFLECTIVE JOURNALING

_____

_____

_____

_____

_____

_____

_____

_____

_____

_____

_____

_____

_____

_____

_____

_____

_____

_____

PSALM 31 ▪ EXODUS 4:10-20 ▪ 1 CORINTHIANS 12:31—13:2 ▪ MARK 9:30-41

MORNING MEDITATIONS

PRAYER—Almighty God, you alone can bring into order all the unruly affections of my life. I pray that you will give me grace to love what you command and desire what you promise so that my heart may be focused where true joy is found. In the name and for the sake of Jesus Christ, I pray. Amen. *JW*

PSALM 31:1-2—In you, O LORD, I seek refuge; do not let me ever be put to shame; in your righteousness deliver me. Incline your ear to me; rescue me speedily. Be a rock of refuge for me, a strong fortress to save me.

EXODUS 4:10-12 *Is It Not I, the Lord?*
Moses said to the LORD, "O my Lord, I have never been eloquent . . . I am slow of speech and slow of tongue." Then the LORD said to him, "Who gives speech to mortals? Who makes them mute or deaf, seeing or blind? Is it not I, the LORD? Now go, and I will . . . teach you what you are to speak."

1 CORINTHIANS 12:31—13:2a, 2d *A Still More Excellent Way*
Strive for the greater gifts. And I will show you a still more excellent way. If I speak in the tongues of mortals and of angels, but do not have love, I am a noisy gong or a clanging cymbal. And if I have prophetic powers . . . but do not have love, I am nothing.

MARK 9:30-41 *Today's Gospel Reading*

> If we can ever get ourselves unhinged from our self-dependency and let our whole weight down on God's love, we can live in the joyful confidence of his will and his work being done in us; and we don't have to have our egos on the line!
>
> REUBEN WELCH, *PREACHING FROM 2 CORINTHIANS*

EVENING REFLECTIONS

PSALM 35:22-24a—You have seen, O LORD; do not be silent! O Lord, do not be far from me! Wake up! Bestir yourself for my defense, for my cause, my God and my Lord! Vindicate me, O LORD, my God, according to your righteousness.

PRAYER—O God, fill my soul with so entire a love for you, that I may love nothing but you. Give me grace to study your knowledge daily, that the more I know you, the more I may love you, through Jesus Christ my Lord. Amen. *JW*

PSALM 121 ▪ EXODUS 5:1—6:13 ▪ 1 CORINTHIANS 14:21-33a, 39-40 ▪ MARK 9:42-50

MORNING MEDITATIONS

PRAYER—O Lord, . . . it is my duty, to love you with all my heart, and with all my strength. I know you are infinitely holy and overflowing in all perfection, and therefore it is my duty to love you. Yet not only my duty, but my joy, in Jesus' name. Amen. *JW*

PSALM 121:1-2, 7—I lift up my eyes to the hills—from where will my help come? My help comes from the Lord, who made heaven and earth . . . The Lord will keep you from all evil; he will keep your life.

EXODUS 6:1, 6 *I Will Redeem You*
Then the Lord said to Moses, "Now you shall see what I will do to Pharaoh: Indeed, by a mighty hand he will let them go . . . I am the Lord, and I will free you from the burdens of the Egyptians and deliver you from slavery to them. I will redeem you with an outstretched arm and with mighty acts of judgment."

1 CORINTHIANS 14:21 *Strange Tongues*
In the law it is written, "By people of strange tongues and by the lips of foreigners I will speak to this people; yet even then they will not listen to me," says the Lord.

MARK 9:42-50 *Today's Gospel Reading*

It is the Spirit of Christ our Lord who gives us freedom, enables us to steadfastly behold Christ, and accomplishes in us inner transformation into Christlikeness. The freedom that is ours through the Spirit of our Lord is both freedom from bondage to the old covenant, that is, from legalism, and freedom in the sense of open and courageous confidence.

REUBEN WELCH, *PREACHING FROM 2 CORINTHIANS*

EVENING REFLECTIONS

PSALM 126:1-3—When the Lord restored the fortunes of Zion, . . . our mouth was filled with laughter, and our tongue with shouts of joy; then it was said among the nations, "The Lord has done great things for them." The Lord has done great things for us, and we rejoiced.

PRAYER—O my Father, my God, I ask you to deliver me from any passion that obstructs my knowledge and love of you. Let none of them find a way into my heart, but instead give me a meek and gentle spirit. Reign in my heart; may I always be your servant and love you entirely, through Christ I pray. Amen. *JW*

PSALM 119:145-176 ▪ **EXODUS 7:1-24** ▪ **2 CORINTHIANS 2:14—3:6** ▪ **MARK 10:1-16**

MORNING MEDITATIONS

PRAYER—O God, fill me with confidence and trust that in knowing your will, I may follow it, and that in following your will, I will find joy, through Jesus Christ, my Lord. Amen.

PSALM 119:145a, 146-147, 174—With my whole heart I cry; answer me, O LORD . . . I cry to you: save me, that I may observe your decrees. I rise before dawn and cry for help; I put my hope in your words . . . I long for your salvation, O Lord, and your law is my delight.

EXODUS 7:2a, 5a, 20b-21a *They Shall Know that I Am the Lord*
"You shall speak all that I command you . . . The Egyptians shall know that I am the LORD" . . . [Moses] lifted up the staff . . . and all the water in the river was turned to blood, and the fish in the river died. The river stank so that the Egyptians could not drink its water.

2 CORINTHIANS 2:14, 17b *We Speak with Sincerity*
But thanks be to God, who in Christ always leads us in triumphal procession, and through us spreads in every place the fragrance that comes from knowing him . . . In Christ we speak as persons of sincerity, as persons sent from God standing in his presence.

MARK 10:1-16 *Today's Gospel Reading*

Resurrection is not God's drawing Jesus back from the tomb. Resurrection is God's going through the tomb. It is God's conquering of death in a way that robs it of its ultimate power over us. In Jesus, God takes to himself the full weight of the finality of death, and then he triumphs over it in the resurrection.   REUBEN WELCH, *PREACHING FROM 2 CORINTHIANS*

EVENING REFLECTIONS

PSALM 130:1-2, 5-6a—Out of the depths I cry to you, O LORD. Lord, hear my voice! Let your ears be attentive to the voice of my supplications! . . . I wait for the LORD, my soul waits, and in his word I hope; my soul waits for the Lord more that those who watch for the morning.

PRAYER—Father, grant me forgiveness of what is past, that in the days to come I may with a pure spirit, do your will—walking humbly with you, showing love to all, and keeping body and soul in sanctification and honor, in Jesus' name. Amen. *JW*

PSALM 132 ▪ EXODUS 7:25—8:19 ▪ 2 CORINTHIANS 3:7-18 ▪ MARK 10:17-31

MORNING MEDITATIONS

PRAYER—O Eternal God, my Savior and Lord, I acknowledge that all I am and all I have is yours. I pray that you will surround me with such a sense of your infinite goodness, that I may return to you all possible love and obedience, through Jesus Christ, Amen. **JW**

PSALM 132:13-16—For the Lord has chosen Zion; he has desired it for his habitation: "This is my resting place forever; here I will reside, for I have desired it. I will abundantly bless its provisions; I will satisfy its poor with bread. Its priests I will clothe with salvation, and its faithful will shout with joy.

EXODUS 8:16a, 17a, 18a, 19a   *The Finger of God*
Then the Lord said to Moses, "Say to Aaron, 'Stretch out your staff and strike the dust'" . . . Aaron . . . struck the dust of the earth, and . . . all the dust of the earth turned into gnats . . . The magicians tried to produce gnats by their secret arts, but they could not . . . And the magicians said to Pharaoh, "This is the finger of God!"

2 CORINTHIANS 3:7-8   *The Ministry of the Spirit Comes in Glory*
Now if the ministry of death, chiseled in letters on stone tablets, came in glory so that the people of Israel could not gaze on Moses' face because of the glory of his face . . . how much more will the ministry of the Spirit come in glory?

MARK 10:17-31   *Today's Gospel Reading*

The new relationship of righteousness does not grow dim and fade. Rules do, systems do, externals do. But life in Jesus doesn't. The glory keeps going on. And it will keep going on forever. That's the promise!   REUBEN WELCH, *PREACHING FROM 2 CORINTHIANS*

EVENING REFLECTIONS

PSALM 140:12-13—I know that the Lord maintains the cause of the needy, and executes justice for the poor. Surely the righteous shall give thanks to your name; the upright shall live in your presence.

PRAYER—Protect me, Lord, as I stay awake; watch over me as I sleep, that awake, I may keep watch with Christ, and asleep, rest in his peace. Amen.

PSALM 22 ▪ EXODUS 9:13-35 ▪ 2 CORINTHIANS 4:1-12 ▪ MARK 10:32-45

MORNING MEDITATIONS

PRAYER—Father in Heaven! You have loved us first; help me never to forget that you are love, so that this sure conviction might triumph in my heart over the seduction of the world, over the anxiety for the future, over the fright of the past, over the distress of the moment. Amen. **Søren Kierkegaard**

PSALM 22:3-5—You are holy, enthroned on the praises of Israel. In you our ancestors trusted; they trusted, and you delivered them. To you they cried, and were saved; in you they trusted, and were not put to shame.

EXODUS 9:27, 29, 30b, 33a, 35 *The Lord Is in the Right*
Pharaoh summoned Moses and Aaron, and said to them, "This time I have sinned; the Lord is in the right, and I and my people are in the wrong". . . Moses said to him . . . "I know that you do not yet fear the Lord God". . . So Moses left Pharaoh . . . So the heart of Pharaoh was hardened, and he would not let the Israelites go, just as the Lord had spoken through Moses.

2 CORINTHIANS 4:3-4 *The God of This World Has Blinded Their Minds*
And even if our gospel is veiled, it is veiled to those who are perishing. In their case the god of this world has blinded the minds of the unbelievers, to keep them from seeing the light of the gospel of the glory of Christ who is the image of God.

MARK 10:32-45 *Today's Gospel Reading*

Because the promise of God that, from mortality and corruption, from this weak and abject state, from dust and ashes, we could become equal to the angels of God seemed incredible to men, he not only made a written covenant . . . but also gave them a Mediator as a pledge of his promise.   ST. AUGUSTINE, *DISCOURSES ON THE PSALMS*

EVENING REFLECTIONS

PSALM 143:1, 7a, 9—Hear my prayer, O Lord; give ear to my supplications in your faithfulness; answer me in your righteousness . . . Answer me quickly, O Lord; my spirit fails . . . Save me, O Lord, . . . I have fled to you for refuge.

PRAYER—Almighty God, your love for us is more than we could ever imagine. Fill our lives with your love, our minds with your thoughts, our mouths with your truth, so that every part of our living is touched by your grace. Amen.

PSALM 144 ▪ EXODUS 10:21—11:10 ▪ 2 CORINTHIANS 4:13-18 ▪ MARK 10:46-52

MORNING MEDITATIONS

PRAYER—Father in Heaven! You have loved us first. Grant that this conviction might discipline my soul so that my heart might remain faithful and sincere in the love which I owe to all those whom you have commanded me to love as I love myself. Amen. **Søren Kierkegaard**

PSALM 144:5, 7-8—Bow your heavens, O LORD, and come down; touch the mountains so that they smoke . . . Stretch out your hand from on high; set me free and rescue me from . . . the hand of aliens, whose mouths speak lies, and whose right hands are false.

EXODUS 11:1a-b, 4-5a, 10b-c   *The Lord Hardened Pharaoh's Heart*
The LORD said to Moses, "I will bring one more plague upon Pharaoh and upon Egypt; afterwards he will let you go from here . . . Moses said, "Thus says the LORD: About midnight I will go out through Egypt. Every firstborn in the land of Egypt shall die" . . . But the LORD hardened Pharaoh's heart, and he did not let the people of Israel go.

2 CORINTHIANS 4:13-14   *I Believed and So I Spoke*
But just as we have the same spirit of faith that is in accordance with scripture—"I believed, and so I spoke"—we also believe, and so we speak, because we know that the one who raised the Lord Jesus will raise us also with Jesus, and will bring us with you into his presence.

MARK 10:46-52   *Today's Gospel Reading*

Come, come, let us go up together to the Mount of Olives. Together, let us meet Christ, who is returning from Bethany and going of his own accord . . . to complete the mystery of our salvation. And so he comes, willingly taking the road to Jerusalem, he who came down from the heights for us, to raise us who lie in the depths to exaltation with him.

ST. ANDREW OF CRETE

EVENING REFLECTIONS

PSALM 43:5—Why are you cast down, O my soul, and why are you disquieted within me? Hope in God; for I shall again praise him, my help and my God.

PRAYER—Teach me, O Lord, to go through all of my activities with a truly devoted heart, so that I may see you in all things . . . Search my motives so that I may never weaken the liberty of spirit which is so necessary for the love of you. Amen. **JW**

WEEK SIX (Holy Week)
Lenten Season

Sunday: The Lord Needs It

Read the Gospel passage from Mark 11:1-11 and the devotional reflection titled "The Lord Needs It," then respond to the discussion prompts in the Reflective Journaling section.

THE MUSIC OF ASHES TO FIRE

Week 6: "The Glory of Dying" (Track 7)

Monday through Saturday of Week 6

IN THE MORNING:

A personal daily devotional guide includes prayer, a reading from the Old Testament, the Psalms, the Epistles, and the Gospel for each day of the week.

This week's readings are from Lamentations, 2 Corinthians, Romans, and the Gospels of Mark and John.

Inspirational quotes from men and women of faith keep us in contact with our shared Christian heritage.

IN THE EVENING:

An evening psalm and prayer become preludes to nighttime rest and renewal.

LENTEN SEASON–WEEK SIX
The Lord Needs It

A devotional reflection based on Mark 11:1-11

*R*ead the Gospel passage first, then the devotional reflection that follows. *The discussion prompts at the end will help prepare you for Sunday school and small-group sessions.*

What else would happen this strange day? It began with the king's royal stablemen arriving a day early leading Uncle Zell's newly acquired high-priced colt. The fence being built in the back pasture would not be finished until tomorrow. Poneus told the men to tie the donkey's foal out front near the road so he could watch him. Last week, his Uncle Zell, a successful businessman, bought the colt from the king's royal stables. He said it was a good way to celebrate his election to the village council. He needed a striking mount for riding into important village meetings. The untrained colt was perfect. The king, himself, often enjoyed riding donkeys. The king believed donkeys were surefooted, loyal creatures. They signified dignity and rank. When the king wanted to communicate his military and political power, he rode his horse. When he wanted to send a message of peace and goodwill, he rode his donkey.

This day was also strange because of all the foot traffic. Normally, a handful of dusty wayfarers hiked the steep seventeen miles from Jericho to Jerusalem. Occasionally a stranger would stop by the house to ask for a drink, but today several thirsty pilgrims had stopped. The strenuous trip, rising over thirty-four hundred feet, demanded six hours of brisk uphill hiking. The steady stream of pilgrims seemed extraordinarily lighthearted, almost giddy with exhilaration. Going to Jerusalem for Passover was exciting but not this exciting. This was indeed a strange day.

Only minutes earlier a bearded traveler had turned off the road, walked to the shady sycamore where Poneus relaxed with friends, greeted them, and asked for a drink.

Poneus half smiled, half scowled, nodded, and motioned for the servant girl to bring the man a drink.

"What is happening out there on the road?" Poneus asked as he watched his servant pass the visitor a skin of freshly drawn cold water from the ancient family well.

The stranger took a long gulping swig, swiped his bearded chin, and said, "Well, I have just witnessed the most amazing thing. This morning Timaeus's son, Bartimaeus, the one who can't see, was begging at his usual spot, when the Nazarene preacher with a huge crowd came out of Jericho. All of a sudden blind Bartimaeus started hollering at the top of his voice, 'Jesus, Son of David, have mercy on me!' Some of us told him to be quiet, but he wouldn't listen. The more we tried to get him to be still, the louder he shouted, 'Son of David, have mercy on me!'

"Somehow in the midst of all the noise Jesus heard him. Jesus stopped. The crowd stopped. Someone told Bartimaeus, 'Get up. Go! He is calling for you.'

"Bartimaeus leaped to his feet and started tapping his way to Jesus. When he got there, Jesus asked, 'What do you want?' 'I want to see!' said Bartimaeus. Jesus said, 'Go, your faith has healed you.' Just like that, Bartimaeus blinked and he could see! [See Mark 10:46-52.]

"Right now, Jesus, his disciples, Bartimaeus, and hundreds are headed this way! They would have been here by now, but the sick keep coming up to him, and Jesus keeps stopping to heal them. Wherever he goes amazing things are happening. Have you heard he brought a dead man back to life? He casts out demons, makes sick people well, the deaf people hear, the lame walk, the blind see. It is indescribable. The crowd is stirred up. They think he is coming to Jerusalem to take charge. He's going to straighten things out. We should make him our king. Herod sure won't like that! This could spell trouble!"

"Hey, what are they doing?" gasped the servant girl pointing to the fence line where the prized colt was tied. Two obviously Galilean men, covered with road dust, had brazenly stepped through the gate, marched straight across the yard, and started untying the trophy donkey.

"What do you think you are doing?" shouted Poneus. Jumping to his feet, he grabbed a stick and quickly crossed the yard to confront the intruders. "This is my uncle's new colt. Why are you untying him?" demanded Poneus. Slowly the Galileans turned to the angry face. Carefully and quietly they repeated exactly what Jesus told them to say, "The Lord needs it and will send it back here shortly" (11:3, NIV).

Stunned, Poneus frowned. The words, "The Lord needs it" baffled him. Poneus blinked then dropped his stick. His friends watched warily. "The Lord needs it"—strange words for a strange day.

The Galileans quietly and quickly untied the colt and led it to the road. A crowd, with Jesus in the middle, had just crested the hill. The disciples twisted their way through the animated throng, peeled off their clothes, and threw them on the colt. Others started throwing their cloaks and spreading leafy branches on the roadway. Then Jesus sat on the donkey. Suddenly the crowd burst out shouting, "Hosanna!" "Save us now, Save, we pray!" "Blessed is he who comes in the name of the Lord!" (v. 9, NIV).

As Poneus watched the spontaneous singing, the emphatic explanation "The Lord needs it!" burned in his heart. "Why," he wondered, "would a conquering king with powers from God ride into the city on a donkey, like a man of peace?" Immediately Poneus remembered prophet Zechariah's words: "Rejoice greatly, O Daughter of Zion! Shout, Daughter of Jerusalem! See, your king comes to you, righteous and having salvation, gentle and riding on a donkey, on a colt, the foal of a donkey" (Zech. 9:9, NIV). Was this miracle worker the One spoken about in prophecy? Could this possibly be Messiah? Poneus pondered these things as he watched the Nazarene Rabbi ride the colt into the city. —WS

After reading the passage from Mark 11:1-11 and the devotional reflection "The Lord Needs It," you may also want to read the following related passages:
Isaiah 50:4-9; Psalm 31:9-16; Philippians 2:5-11

The discussion prompts that follow will help prepare you to participate in your Sunday school class or small-group study. Use your Reflective Journaling section to record any other insights that come to you as you read the Gospel lesson and the devotional reflection.

DISCUSSION PROMPT NO. 1: MARK 11

Jesus sent his disciples to bring him a colt, and the people let them take it. How might Jesus want to use your resources for him?

DISCUSSION PROMPT NO. 2: MARK 11

What was the significance of Jesus riding on a colt? (See Zech. 9:9.)

DISCUSSION PROMPT NO. 3: MARK 11

"Hosanna" was both a cry for salvation and of praise. Why do you think the crowd shouted "Hosanna"?

DISCUSSION PROMPT NO. 4: MARK 11

The people spread their clothes on the ground and waved branches to honor Jesus. What are some ways we show him honor today?

DISCUSSION PROMPT NO. 5: DEVOTIONAL REFLECTION

If the Lord asked for something that belonged to you, do you think you would be willing to release it to him for his purposes? Explain.

REFLECTIVE JOURNALING

_____

_____

_____

_____

_____

_____

_____

_____

_____

_____

_____

_____

_____

_____

_____

_____

_____

_____

_____

PSALM 51:1-18 ▪ LAMENTATIONS 1:1-2, 6-12 ▪ 2 CORINTHIANS 1:1-7 ▪ MARK 11:12-25

MORNING MEDITATIONS

PRAYER—O God, let me live this whole day for the purpose for which it was intended—in works of mercy and necessity; in prayer, praise and meditation; and let the words of my mouth and the meditation of my heart be always acceptable in your sight. Amen. **JW**

PSALM 51:17-19a—The sacrifice acceptable to God is a broken spirit; a broken and contrite heart, O God, you will not despise. Do good to Zion in your good pleasure; rebuild the walls of Jerusalem, then you will delight in right sacrifices.

LAMENTATIONS 1:1a-b, 6a, 12a-b How Lonely Sits the City
How lonely sits the city that once was full of people! How like a widow she has become, she that was great among the nations . . . From daughter Zion has departed all her majesty . . . Is it nothing to you, all you who pass by? Look and see if there is any sorrow like my sorrow.

2 CORINTHIANS 1:3, 5 The Sufferings of Christ Are Abundant
Blessed be the God and Father of our Lord Jesus Christ, the Father of mercies and the God of all consolation . . . For just as the sufferings of Christ are abundant for us, so also our consolation is abundant through Christ.

MARK 11:12-25 Today's Gospel Reading

The rejection and crucifixion of Jesus means . . . the era of the Temple is over. A new worship is being introduced, in a Temple not built with human hands. This Temple is his body, this Risen One . . . [Jesus] himself is the new Temple of redeemed humanity.

JOSEPH RATZINGER, *JESUS OF NAZARETH*

EVENING REFLECTIONS

PSALM 69:16-18—Answer me, O LORD, for your steadfast love is good; according to your abundant mercy, turn to me. Do not hide your face from your servant, for I am in distress—make haste to answer me. Draw near to me, redeem me, set me free because of my enemies.

PRAYER—Christ be with me, Christ within me, Christ behind me, Christ before me, Christ beside me, Christ to win me, Christ to comfort and restore me. Christ beneath me, Christ above me, Christ in quiet, Christ in danger, Christ in hearts of all who love me, Christ in mouth of friend and stranger. *From St. Patrick's Breastplate*

PSALM 12 ▪ LAMENTATIONS 1:17-22 ▪ 2 CORINTHIANS 1:8-22 ▪ MARK 11:27-33

MORNING MEDITATIONS

PRAYER—Eternal and Merciful Father, I know you have created me, and that I have neither being nor blessing but what is the effect of your power and goodness. I know that you are the end for which I was created, and that I can expect no happiness but in you. So, I bless your name. Amen. *JW*

PSALM 12:1, 7a—Help, O LORD, for there is no longer anyone who is godly; the faithful have disappeared from humankind . . . [Yet] you, O LORD, will protect us.

LAMENTATIONS 1:17a, c, 18b, 20a *Behold My Suffering*
Zion stretches out her hands, but there is no one to comfort her . . . Jerusalem has become a filthy thing among [the people] . . . Hear, all you peoples, and behold my suffering; my young women and young men have gone into captivity . . . See, O LORD, how distressed I am.

2 CORINTHIANS 1:8b-9 *We Rely on God*
For we were so utterly, unbearably crushed that we despaired of life itself. Indeed, we felt that we had received the sentence of death so that we would rely not on ourselves but on God who raises the dead.

MARK 11:27-33 *Today's Gospel Reading*

If we start with Jesus, we find that the incarnation and the atonement were possible because human persons were made in the *imago Dei,* in the image of divine persons . . . His willingness to assume into himself all of the sin and hurt of the world enable the possibility for fellowship between God and human persons to be restored.

DENNIS KINLAW, *LET'S START WITH JESUS*

EVENING REFLECTIONS

PSALM 94:16, 22—Who rises up for me against the wicked? . . . If the LORD had not been my help, my soul would soon have lived in the land of silence . . . But the Lord has become my stronghold, and my God the rock of my refuge.

PRAYER—O Christ Jesus, when . . . I feel my weakness and helplessness, give me the sense of your . . . love, and your strength. Help me to have perfect trust in your protecting love and strengthening power, so that nothing may frighten or worry us; for in living close to you I shall see your hand, your purpose, your will through all things. ***St. Ignatius of Loyola***

**PSALM 55 ▪ LAMENTATIONS 2:1-9 ▪ 2 CORINTHIANS 1:23—2:11 ▪
MARK 12:1-11**

MORNING MEDITATIONS

PRAYER—My Lord and my God, let it be the one desire of my heart to live as my Master lived, whose whole life declared, "Father, not my will [but] your will be done." Give me grace today to follow his pattern and to walk in his steps. Give me grace to take up my cross daily and bear any hardship for his sake. Amen. **JW**

PSALM 55:4a, 5a, 16-17—My heart is in anguish within me . . . Fear and trembling come upon me . . . But I call upon God, and the LORD will save me. Evening and morning and at noon I utter my complaint and moan, and he will hear my voice.

LAMENTATIONS 2:5 *Mourning and Lamentation in Judah*
The Lord has become like an enemy; he has destroyed Israel. He has destroyed all its palaces, laid in ruins its strongholds, and multiplied in daughter Judah mourning and lamentation.

2 CORINTHIANS 2:4 *With Many Tears*
I wrote you out of much distress and anguish of heart and with many tears, not to cause you pain, but to let you know the abundant love that I have for you.

MARK 12:1-11 *Today's Gospel Reading*

Jesus himself is the presence of the living God. God and man, God and the world, touch one another in him . . . In his self-offering on the Cross, Jesus brings all the sin of the world deep with the love of God, and wipes it away. Accepting the Cross, entering into fellowship with Christ, means entering the realm of transformation.

JOSEPH RATZINGER, *JESUS OF NAZARETH*

EVENING REFLECTIONS

PSALM 74:18a, 20a, 21-22a—Remember this, O LORD, how the enemy scoffs . . . Have regard for your covenant . . . Do not let the downtrodden be put to shame; let the poor and needy praise your name. Rise up, O God, plead your cause.

PRAYER—O God, deliver me from a slothful mind, from lukewarm affections, and all dejections of spirit. These faults can only deaden my love for you. In your mercy, free my heart to become passionate and cheerful so that I can vigorously pursue whatever you have for me to do and be fervent in my obedience to your holy love. Amen. **JW**

PSALM 102 ▪ LAMENTATIONS 2:10-18 ▪ 1 CORINTHIANS 11:27-32 ▪ MARK 14:12-25

MORNING MEDITATIONS

PRAYER—Lord Jesus, abject, unknown, and despised, have mercy upon me, and let me not be ashamed to follow you. O Jesus, betrayed and sold at a vile price, have mercy on me and make me content to serve you as Master. O Jesus, blasphemed, accused, and wrongfully condemned, have mercy on me, and teach me to endure the contradiction of sinners. Amen. **JW**

PSALM 102:1-2—Hear my prayer, O LORD; let my cry come to you. Do not hide your face from me in the day of my distress. Incline your ear to me; answer me speedily in the day when I call.

LAMENTATIONS 2:10a-b, 13a, c   Vast as the Sea Is Your Ruin
The elders of daughter Zion sit on the ground in silence; they have thrown dust on their heads and put on sackcloth . . . What can I say for you, to what compare you, O daughter Jerusalem? . . . For vast as the sea is your ruin; who can heal you?

1 CORINTHIANS 11:27-28a, 29   Examine Yourselves
Whoever, therefore, eats the bread or drinks the cup of the Lord in an unworthy manner will be answerable for the body and blood of the Lord. Examine yourselves . . . For all who eat and drink without discerning the body, eat and drink judgment against themselves.

MARK 14:12-25   Today's Gospel Reading

The window of the incarnation and the cross gives us a picture of the inner being of God as a communion of free, other-oriented persons living in a dialogue of self-giving love. This God, Jesus insists, is the God of Israel who called himself holy and commanded us to be the same.   DENNIS KINLAW, *LET'S START WITH JESUS*

EVENING REFLECTIONS

PSALM 142:5—I cry to you, O LORD; I say, "You are my refuge, my portion in the land of the living."

PRAYER—My Lord and my God, you see my heart; and my desires are not hidden from you. I am encouraged and strengthened by your goodness to me today. I want to be yours and yours alone. O my God, my Savior, my Sanctifier, hear me, help me, and show mercy to me for Jesus Christ's sake. Amen. **JW**

PSALM 22 ▪ LAMENTATIONS 3:1-9, 19-33 ▪ 1 PETER 1:10-20 ▪ JOHN 13:36-38

MORNING MEDITATIONS

PRAYER—O Jesus, clothed with our reproach and shame, have mercy upon me, and let me not seek glory for myself. O Jesus, insulted, mocked, scourged, and bathed in blood, have mercy upon me, and let me run with patience the race set before me. Amen. *JW*

PSALM 22:23-24—You who fear the LORD, praise him! All you offspring of Jacob, glorify him; stand in awe of him, all you offspring of Israel! For he did not despise or abhor the affliction of the afflicted; he did not hide his face from me, but heard when I cried to him.

LAMENTATIONS 3:19, 21-23, 31 *Great Is Your Faithfulness*
The thought of my affliction and my homelessness is wormwood and gall! . . . But this I call to mind, and therefore I have hope: The steadfast love of the LORD never ceases, his mercies never come to an end; they are new every morning, great is your faithfulness . . . For the Lord will not reject forever.

1 PETER 1:18-19 *The Precious Blood*
You know that you were ransomed from the futile ways inherited from your ancestors, not with perishable things like silver or gold, but with the precious blood of Christ, like that of a lamb without defect or blemish.

JOHN 13:36-38 *Today's Gospel Reading*

In the Cross of Jesus, what the animal sacrifices had sought in vain to achieve actually occurred: atonement was made for the world. The "Lamb of God" took upon himself the sins of the world and wiped them away. God's relationship to the world, formerly distorted by sin, was now renewed. Reconciliation had been accomplished.

JOSEPH RATZINGER, *JESUS OF NAZARETH*

EVENING REFLECTIONS

PSALM 40:1, 13, 17b—I waited patiently for the LORD; he inclined to me and heard my cry . . . Be pleased, O LORD, to deliver me; O LORD, make haste to help me . . . You are my help and my deliverer; do not delay, O my God.

READ: JOHN 19:38-42

PSALM 88 ▪ LAMENTATIONS 3:37-58 ▪ HEBREWS 4:1-16 ▪ ROMANS 8:1-11

MORNING MEDITATIONS

PRAYER—O Jesus, crowned with thorns, burdened with my sin, overwhelmed with injuries, hanging on the accursed tree, bowing the head, surrendering your life to death, have mercy on me and conform me to your holy, humble, suffering spirit. Amen. *JW*

PSALM 88:1-2a, 3a, 6, 11a—O LORD, God of my salvation, when, at night, I cry out in your presence, let my prayer come before you . . .For my soul is full of troubles . . . You have put me in the depths of the Pit, in the regions dark and deep . . . Is your steadfast love declared in the grave?

LAMENTATIONS 3:55-57   *Do Not Fear*
I called on your name, O LORD, from the depths of the pit; you heard my plea, "Do not close your ear to my cry for help, but give me relief!" You came near when I called on you; you said, "Do not fear!"

HEBREWS 4:15-16   *Mercy and Grace in Time of Need*
For we do not have a high priest who is unable to sympathize with our weaknesses, but we have one who in every respect has been tested as we are, yet without sin. Let us therefore approach the throne of grace with boldness, so that we may receive mercy and find grace to help in time of need.

THERE IS NO READING OF THE GOSPEL TODAY.

His sacrifice was not forced upon him. It would be a voluntary act, a sacrifice of double-edged love. He wanted to please his Father, and he loved the world . . . Jesus *chose* to die; he was no martyr. His life was not taken from him; he gave it. This fact makes the cross a window through which we so clearly can see the nature of God.

DENNIS KINLAW, *LET'S START WITH JESUS*

EVENING REFLECTIONS

PSALM 27:13-14—I believe that I shall see the goodness of the LORD in the land of the living. Wait for the LORD; be strong, and let your heart take courage; wait for the LORD!

READ: ROMANS 8:1-11

WEEK ONE
EASTER SEASON

Ashes to Fire Week 7

Sunday: Seeing Is Believing!

Read the Gospel passage from John 20:1-18 and the devotional reflection titled "Seeing Is Believing!" then respond to the discussion prompts in the Reflective Journaling section.

THE MUSIC OF ASHES TO FIRE

Week 7: "No Grave" (Track 8)

Monday through Saturday of Easter Season Week 1

IN THE MORNING:

A personal daily devotional guide includes prayer, a reading from the Old Testament, the Psalms, the Epistles, and the Gospel for each day of the week.

This week's readings are from Exodus, 1 Corinthians, and the Gospels of Mark, Matthew, and Luke.

Inspirational quotes from men and women of faith keep us in contact with our shared Christian heritage.

IN THE EVENING:

An evening psalm and prayer become preludes to nighttime rest and renewal.

EASTER SEASON–WEEK ONE
Seeing Is Believing!

A devotional reflection based on John 20:1-18

*R*ead the Gospel passage first, then the devotional reflection that follows. The discussion prompts at the end will help prepare you for Sunday school and small-group sessions.

Fear! Uncertainty! Confusion! Desperation! It is all in those first eighteen verses of chapter 20 in John's Gospel. You can feel it in the words. You can see it in the faces as you imagine yourself there, suddenly confronted with the unexpected, the irrational, the unbelievable! It begins where we all begin when our deepest longings have been crushed, when our certainties have been assaulted, with our worst fears suddenly confronting us. Wasn't killing him enough for them! Why further wound by desecrating the body?

Mary Magdalene had come with the most committed of intentions. Not content to allow the indignity of death by crucifixion to have the last word, she was determined to do her part to provide at least a modicum of honor to the body of the One who had enabled her utter and complete transformation. She could do no less!

She approached the grave where the body had been hastily placed; and seeing the seal broken, the tomb open, she seems not to have taken the time to peer in. Rather, in confusion and fear she ran, desperate for help, to find Peter and John.

In moments like this we have a hard time remembering what should have registered when critically important words were spoken. After all, it was not as if they had not been told. How many times and in how many ways had he told them? "The Son of Man will be betrayed. They will kill him. On the third day he will be raised."

But now, in the face of another unexpected turn of events—there had been so many of them—they knew only confused uncertainty.

Lumbering Simon Peter was outrun by the younger John, who stopped respectfully outside the tomb, peering in at what was not yet clear. It was the always impetuous Simon who dove into the tomb, not content with protocols or respectful distance. Then John stepped in.

How is it that a dawning realization that defies all reason can come so suddenly? John saw and *believed*! In spite of the fact that they did not yet understand from the Scriptures that Jesus should be raised from the dead, John somehow understood anyway!

What makes such belief possible? How can one suddenly just *know*?

He *saw*!

We are often so jaded by our innate pessimism that we can miss the subtle movements of God's grace. It seems to come with age and experience. That wonderful capability to believe, so normal to the life of most healthy children, is eroded by our exposure to the cynicism and suspicion of the cultures around us. We lose our ability to "see" the intrusions on our reality that become potential moments of encounter with the miraculous.

No one had to explain it to John. No scriptural "proofs" were necessary to him in that dawning awareness. It suddenly was clear, at a level that must have been a surprise even to him. He just *knew*!

And Mary? It is fascinating to imagine that exchange. A figure appears unexpectedly, only confounding her further. She had just seen angels, if that is what they were! What was she to believe? She had been so sure he was the Anointed One! Oh, the horror of his suffering and death. And then the dismay at discovering an empty tomb. John's sudden delight seemed so out of place in the face of everything else that had happened.

It was when he called her by name that she knew. It was like all the music of the universe was concentrated in that one word: *Mary*!

How is it that a word can reverse the order of the universe? Why do you sometimes have no explanation as to how you know? You just *know*! She would have known that voice anywhere, calling her name as only he could do it. When your life has been rearranged by the way a voice calls your name, you just know. Without need for explanation she addresses him with that title of intimate respect and adoration that expressed more in a word than a thousand pages could accomplish: "Teacher!" (v. 16).

What about Simon Peter? No further word is given us by John's Gospel as to how he knew. "The disciples returned to their homes" (v. 10). John returned believing. But what about Simon?

We have a clue in Luke's Gospel. Late in the day, when the two who had encountered the Risen Lord on the road to Emmaus reached the room where the disciples had gathered, the word was out: "The Lord has risen indeed, and he has appeared to Simon!" (24:34). No word about how it happened. No account as to what was said. What goes on between a deserter and the Savior is none of our business. But what we know is that whatever occurred in that encounter changed the world. Simon *knew*! Oh, the wonder of Easter when you *know*! —JM

> ### After reading the passage from John 20:1-18 and the devotional reflection "Seeing Is Believing!" you may also want to read the following related passages:
> Acts 10:34-43; Psalm 118:1-2, 14-24; 1 Corinthians 15:1-11

The discussion prompts that follow will help prepare you to participate in your Sunday school class or small-group study. Use your Reflective Journaling section to record any other insights that come to you as you read the Gospel lesson and the devotional reflection.

DISCUSSION PROMPT NO. 1: JOHN 20

What do you think Mary's, Peter's, and the other disciple's thoughts and feelings were when they believed Jesus' body had been taken away with the burial wrappings?

DISCUSSION PROMPT NO. 2: JOHN 20

Why do you think Mary did not recognize Jesus right away?

DISCUSSION PROMPT NO. 3: JOHN 20

What might Mary's thoughts and feelings have been when she realized she was talking to Jesus?

DISCUSSION PROMPT NO. 4: JOHN 20

Mary witnessed to the disciples that she had seen the Lord. What, or how, can we tell others about our personal encounters with Christ?

DISCUSSION PROMPT NO. 5: DEVOTIONAL REFLECTION

The writer observes, "It was when he called her by name that she knew." Has there been a time of confusion in your life when you have been aware of the Lord's presence in a unique way? What happened?

REFLECTIVE JOURNALING

_____

_____

_____

_____

_____

_____

_____

_____

_____

_____

_____

_____

_____

_____

_____

_____

_____

_____

_____

_____

_____

PSALM 93 ▪ **EXODUS 12:14-27** ▪ **1 CORINTHIANS 15:1-11** ▪ **MARK 16:1-8**

MORNING MEDITATIONS

PRAYER—O God, by my love for you may my soul be fixed against its tendency to be inconstant. Reduce to indifference anything that is not pleasing in your sight. May this holy flame always warm my heart, that I may serve you with all my might, and consume all selfish desires that I may possess a holy regard for you alone. Amen. *JW*

PSALM 93:1a, c, 2, 5b—The Lord is king, he is robed in majesty . . . He has established the world; it shall never be moved; your throne is established from of old; you are from everlasting . . . holiness befits your house, O Lord, forevermore.

EXODUS 12:23b, 24, 26-27a *The Lord Will Pass Over*
When [the Lord] sees the blood on the lintel and on the two doorposts, the Lord will pass over, . . . You shall observe this rite as a perpetual ordinance for you and your children . . . And when your children ask you, "What do you mean by this observance?" you shall say, "It is the passover sacrifice to the Lord."

1 CORINTHIANS 15:3-4 *He Was Buried, He Was Raised*
For I handed on to you as of first importance what I in turn had received; that Christ died for our sins in accordance with the scriptures, and that he was buried, and that he was raised on the third day in accordance with the scriptures.

MARK 16:1-8 *Today's Gospel Reading*

I am your forgiveness, the pasch of your salvation, the lamb slain for you; it is I who am your ransom, your life, your resurrection, your light, your salvation, your king. I am bringing you to the heights of heaven, I will show you the Father who is from all eternity, I will raise you up with my right hand. ST. MELITO OF SARDIS, *HOMILY 100-102*

EVENING REFLECTIONS

PSALM 66:19-20—But truly God has listened; he has given heed to the words of my prayer. Blessed be God, because he has not rejected my prayer or removed his steadfast love from me.

PRAYER—Lord, now that we have come to the setting of the sun and see the evening light, we give praise to God: Father, Son and Holy Spirit. Worthy are you at all times to be worshipped with holy voices, O Risen Christ and giver of life; therefore the world glorifies you. Amen. *JW*

PSALM 103 ▪ EXODUS 12:28-42 ▪ 1 CORINTHIANS 15:12-28 ▪ MARK 16:9-20

MORNING MEDITATIONS

PRAYER—O Lord, you did not please yourself even though all things were created for your pleasure. Let some portion of your Spirit descend on me, so that I may deny myself and follow you, in Jesus' name, Amen. **JW**

PSALM 103:17, 19, 22b—The steadfast love of the Lord is from everlasting to everlasting on those who fear him, and his righteousness to children's children . . . The Lord has established his throne in the heavens, and his kingdom rules over all. . . . Bless the Lord, O my soul.

EXODUS 12:41-42 *A Night of Vigil*
At the end of four hundred thirty years, on that very day, all the companies of the Lord went out from the land of Egypt. That was for the Lord a night of vigil, to bring them out of the land of Egypt. That same night is a vigil to be kept for the Lord by all the Israelites throughout their generations.

1 CORINTHIANS 15:22-24a, 25 *Christ the First Fruits*
For as all die in Adam, so all will be made alive in Christ. But each in his own order: Christ the first fruits, then at his coming those who belong to Christ. Then comes the end, when he hands over the kingdom to God the Father . . . For he must reign until he has put all his enemies under his feet.

MARK 16:9-20 *Today's Gospel Reading*

Armed with no supernatural equipment, Jesus had conquered man's last enemy, death. He had shown beyond any possible doubt that the victory was complete. To live again was no longer a pious hope or a wishful thought; it was a certainty.

J. B. PHILLIPS, *RING OF TRUTH*

EVENING REFLECTIONS

PSALM 111:2a, 6-7—Great are the works of the Lord . . . He has shown his people the power of his works, in giving them the heritage of the nations. The works of his hands are faithful and just; all his precepts are trustworthy.

PRAYER—My Father, my God, I am in your hand; and may I rejoice above all things in simply being there. Do with me what seems good to you; just let me love you with all my heart, mind, soul, and strength. Amen. **JW**

**PSALM 99 ▪ EXODUS 12:40-51 ▪ 1 CORINTHIANS 15:30-42 ▪
MATTHEW 28:1-16**

MORNING MEDITATIONS

PRAYER—O Lord, you have set before us the great hope that your kingdom shall come on earth, and have taught us to pray for its coming; give us grace to discern the signs of its dawning, and to work for the perfect day when your will shall be done on earth as it is in heaven, in the name of Jesus, I pray. Amen. **JW**

PSALM 99:5-6a, 7—Extol the LORD our God, worship at his footstool. Holy is he! Moses and Aaron were among his priests . . . He spoke to them in the pillar of cloud; they kept his decrees, and the statutes that he gave them.

EXODUS 12:43a, 47, 50-51   Out of Egypt
The LORD said to Moses and Aaron: This is the ordinance for the passover . . . The whole congregation of Israel shall celebrate it. . . . All the Israelites did just as the LORD had commanded Moses and Aaron. That very day the LORD brought the Israelites out of the land of Egypt.

1 CORINTHIANS 15:35a, 36-37a, 42   What Is Raised Is Imperishable
"How are the dead raised?" . . . What you sow does not come to life unless it dies. And as for what you sow, you do not sow the body that is to be, but a bare seed . . . So it is with the resurrection of the dead. What is sown is perishable, what is raised is imperishable.

MATTHEW 28:1-16   Today's Gospel Reading

"I am dying," said the Lord, "for all men, so that through me all may have life; by my flesh I have redeemed the flesh of all men. For in my death, death will die, and fallen human nature will rise again with me." There was never any other way to destroy the one who had the power of death, and therefore death itself. Christ had to give himself up for us all.   ST. CYRIL OF ALEXANDER, *COMMENTARY ON JOHN'S GOSPEL*

EVENING REFLECTIONS

PSALM 115:9-10a, 12a, 13—O Israel, trust in the LORD! He is their help and their shield. O house of Aaron, trust in the LORD . . . The LORD has been mindful of us . . . he will bless those who fear the LORD, both small and great.

PRAYER—O Lord, visit this place I pray, and drive far from it all the snares of the enemy; may your holy angels dwell with me and guard me in peace, and may your blessings rest upon all of us always; through Jesus Christ, our Lord. Amen. **JW**

THURSDAY

**PSALM 147 ▪ EXODUS 13:3-10 ▪ 1 CORINTHIANS 15:42-50 ▪
MATTHEW 28:16-20**

MORNING MEDITATIONS

PRAYER—Eternal God, my Sovereign Lord, I acknowledge all I am, all I have is yours. I humbly thank you for all the blessings you have bestowed upon me—for creating me in your own image, for redeeming me by the death of your blessed Son, and for the assistance of the Holy Spirit. Amen. *JW*

PSALM 147:1a-b, 15, 19—Praise the Lord! How good it is to sing praises to our God . . . He sends out his command to the earth; his word runs swiftly . . . He declares his word to Jacob, his statutes and ordinances to Israel.

EXODUS 13:3, 7a, 8 *What the Lord Did for Me*
Moses said to the people, "Remember this day on which you came out of Egypt, out of the house of slavery . . . Unleavened bread shall be eaten for seven days . . . You shall tell your child on that day, 'It is because of what the LORD did for me when I came out of Egypt.'"

1 CORINTHIANS 15:45, 47, 49 *We Bear His Image*
"The first man, Adam, became a living being"; the last Adam became a life-giving spirit . . . The first man was from the earth, a man of dust; the second man is from heaven . . . Just as we have borne the image of the man of dust, we will also bear the image of the man of heaven.

MATTHEW 28:16-20 *Today's Gospel Reading*

> I contend that the historicity [of the Gospels] does matter . . . [The resurrection] was no "cunningly devised fable" but an historic irruption of God into human history which gave birth to a young church so sturdy that the pagan world could not stifle or destroy it.
>
> J. B. PHILLIPS, *RING OF TRUTH*

EVENING REFLECTIONS

PSALM 148:11-13—Kings of the earth and all peoples, princes and all rulers of the earth! Young men and women alike, old and young together! Let them praise the name of the LORD, for his name alone is exalted: his glory is above earth and heaven.

PRAYER—O God, as darkness falls you renew your promise to reveal the light of your presence. May your Word be a lantern to my feet and a light unto my path that I may walk as a child of light and sing your praise throughout the world, in Jesus' name. Amen. *JW*

**PSALM 136 ▪ EXODUS 13:1-2, 11-16 ▪ 1 CORINTHIANS 15:51-58 ▪
LUKE 24:1-12**

MORNING MEDITATIONS

PRAYER—Almighty God, I bless you from my heart. O Savior of the World . . . Light of Light . . . you have overcome death, and you sit at the right hand of the Father. Be today my light and peace and make me a new creature, through Christ my Lord. Amen. **JW**

PSALM 136:1, 10a, 11a, 12a—O give thanks to the LORD, for he is good, for his steadfast love endures forever . . . who struck Egypt through their firstborn . . . and brought Israel out from among them . . . with a strong hand and an outstretched arm.

EXODUS 13:1-2a, 14 *By Strength of Hand*
The LORD said to Moses: Consecrate to me all the firstborn . . . When in the future your child asks you, "What does this mean?" you shall answer, "By strength of hand the LORD brought us out of Egypt, from the house of slavery."

1 CORINTHIANS 15:54d, 56-58 *Victory Through Our Lord*
"Death has been swallowed up in victory" . . . The sting of death is sin, and the power of sin is the law. But thanks be to God, who gives us the victory through our Lord Jesus Christ. Therefore, my beloved, be steadfast, immovable, always excelling in the work of the Lord.

LUKE 24:1-12 *Today's Gospel Reading*

The Egyptians . . . who stand for darkness and suffering, are an apt symbol for the sins that harass us . . . The liberation of the children of Israel, and the journey by which they were led to the promised homeland, correspond to the mystery of our redemption, through which we make our way to the brightness of our heavenly home.

ST. BEDE, *COMMENTARY ON 1 PETER*

EVENING REFLECTIONS

PSALM 118:15a, 17, 24—There are glad songs of victory in the tents of the righteous . . . I shall not die, but I shall live, and recount the deeds of the LORD . . . This is the day that the Lord has made; let us rejoice and be glad in it.

PRAYER—Merciful God, whatever you may deny me, do not deny me of your love. Save me from the idolatry of loving the world, or any of the things of the world. Let me never love any creature, but for your sake and in subordination to your love. Take full possession of my heart, raise your throne in it, and rule there as you do in heaven. Amen. **JW**

**PSALM 145 ▪ EXODUS 13:17—14:4 ▪ 2 CORINTHIANS 4:16—5:10 ▪
MARK 12:18-27**

MORNING MEDITATIONS

PRAYER—O God, I bless you that even after many refusals of your grace, you still had patience with me. You have preserved me through the night, and given me yet another day to live in repentant faith. Accept my thanks and praise. Amen. *JW*

PSALM 145:10-11, 13a-b—All your works shall give thanks to you, O Lord, and all your faithful shall bless you. They shall speak of the glory of your kingdom, and tell of your power . . . Your kingdom is an everlasting kingdom, and your dominion endures throughout all generations.

EXODUS 13:21; 14:1, 4 *Lead Along the Way*
The Lord went in front of them in a pillar of cloud by day, to lead them along the way, and in a pillar of fire by night, to give them light . . . Then the Lord said to Moses . . . I will harden Pharaoh's heart, and he will pursue [you], so that I will gain glory for myself . . . and the Egyptians shall know that I am the Lord.

2 CORINTHIANS 4:16-17 *An Eternal Weight of Glory*
So we do not lose heart. Even though our outer nature is wasting away, our inner nature is being renewed day by day. For this slight momentary affliction is preparing us for an eternal weight of glory beyond all measure.

MARK 12:18-27 *Today's Gospel Reading*

It makes a whole world of difference when we believe that God, the whole unimaginable power, love, and wisdom behind everything, is not merely on our side but actually *at work* in our hearts and minds.   J. B. PHILLIPS, *RING OF TRUTH*

EVENING REFLECTIONS

PSALM 104:31, 33—May the glory of the Lord endure forever; may the Lord rejoice in his works . . . I will sing to the Lord as long as I live; I will sing praise to my God while I have being.

PRAYER—High King of Heaven, though I live on earth, I desire your will to be done in my life as it is done in heaven. I will join my song with those of saints and angels in a hymn of unending praise: Holy, holy, holy is the Lord; heaven and earth are full of your glory. Glory to you, O Lord. Amen. *JW*

WEEK TWO
EASTER SEASON

Ashes to Fire Week 8

Sunday: Believing Is Seeing!

Read the Gospel passage from John 20:19-31 and the devotional reflection titled "Believing Is Seeing!" then respond to the discussion prompts in the Reflective Journaling section.

THE MUSIC OF ASHES TO FIRE

Week 8: "The Church's One Foundation" (Track 9)

Monday through Saturday of Easter Season Week 2

IN THE MORNING:

A personal daily devotional guide includes prayer, a reading from the Old Testament, the Psalms, the Epistles, and the Gospel for each day of the week.

This week's readings are from Exodus, I Peter, and the Gospel of John.

Inspirational quotes from men and women of faith keep us in contact with our shared Christian heritage.

IN THE EVENING:

An evening psalm and prayer become preludes to nighttime rest and renewal.

Easter Season—Week Two
Believing Is Seeing!

A devotional reflection based on John 20:19-31

*R*ead the Gospel passage first, then the devotional reflection that follows. The discussion prompts at the end will help prepare you for Sunday school and small-group sessions.

Wouldn't it seem that if you had gathered to celebrate the resurrection of Jesus, locking the door for fear of the Jews was unnecessary? Given what those on the inside now knew, it should be those on the outside who would want the doors locked. Everything they had done to put an end to this threat to the religious and political establishment had utterly failed. Their ultimate weapon had failed—miserably failed. Death was no longer final! Life had broken out in the face of all deathliness and oppression.

But somehow, lurking in the back of the minds of his followers who had *only heard* was the desire to "cover all the bases." Just in case Herod had heard . . . Just in case Pilate was wondering what on earth was going on . . . "Lock those doors. Have someone watching through the peephole."

Then, without a word—he was there! No noise. No opened door. He was just *there*. And suddenly, quivering hope had become glorious reality!

No one had ever been able to speak peace as he had done. Remember the storm? They had talked about it for months. "Don't be afraid," he would say at other times, and in his presence, fear would vanish like mist in sunshine. There he was again, and with that word, "Shalom," peace seemed to invade the room (see John 20:19).

As if to assure them in every way possible, he showed them his hands and side. It was obvious! No more question about it. All you had to do was see him, and it was like the questions never existed.

But what if you have not seen him? What good does it do to just hear about this incredible occurrence? It just doesn't happen like that. We all know it! Death is death, and death is final. All the pious blather about life after death? We know better! The reality is, and has always been, that there is death after life. That is the way life works. "Life," as one man has said, "is a terminal disease."

It sort of makes the words of Thomas more understandable. "Not until I see him! None of this wishful thinking for me. It's delusional, that's what it is!" Or maybe it was only desperate hope. Not the kind that anchors on the promises, but hope that hangs on despite all the contradictions, believing, yet not willing to put all its weight down on it. You desperately want it to be true, you are just not sure.

There may be a painfully pointed truth in the words of Thomas. "Unless I can touch him, I *will not* believe" (see v. 25). But suddenly, there he is again! How does he do that? He is just there! And in words directed straight to the heart of struggling Thomas, Jesus invites him to touch him, to place his fingers on those nail scarred hands, to thrust his hand into that wounded side.

For Thomas it was more than he could stand. Now on his face, he cries out in agonized confession and worships.

What does it take for us to "see"? Why do we so often demand our own private proof? How have we developed such resistance to realities that are greater than that which we so often think of as "tangible"? Could it be that our loss of wonder, our inability to be open to divine surprises, blinds us to the greater realities that are all around us?

"Thomas, you have come to believe because you see. But what a loss! You could have seen so much sooner and known so much more" (see v. 29). The greater joy is ours who have become convinced beyond any need for proof. We know! And what we know makes all the difference.

I was in a fascinating conversation with my son, a pastor. We were talking about various stumbling blocks to belief, especially as it relates to the miracles of Jesus: His walking on the water, healing the diseased, giving sight to the blind, and calming the sea. Wanting some kind of assurance that the younger generation was not averse to believing in the miracles of Jesus, I was asking him if he really believed in those occurrences.

Looking me straight in the eye, he said with conviction, "Dad, when you believe in the resurrection, you can believe in anything!"

He has seen it. Now anything is possible. Lives can be rearranged. Homes can be saved. Churches can burn with a holy passion! When you see it, you can't help but believe. It follows as surely as sunshine follows rain, and it always does.

Happy Easter, again! —JM

**After reading the passage from John 20:19-31
and the devotional reflection "Believing Is Seeing!"
you may also want to read the following
related passages:**

Acts 4:32-35; Psalm 133; and 1 John 1:1—2:2

The discussion prompts that follow will help prepare you to participate in your Sunday school class or small-group study. Use your Reflective Journaling section to record any other insights that come to you as you read the Gospel lesson and the devotional reflection.

DISCUSSION PROMPT NO. 1: JOHN 20

Why do you think Jesus' first words to the disciples were, "Peace be with you" (v. 19)?

DISCUSSION PROMPT NO. 2: JOHN 20

Why do you think Thomas wanted hard evidence to believe? Was this appropriate or inappropriate? Explain.

DISCUSSION PROMPT NO. 3: JOHN 20

Why do you think Jesus said those who have not seen him, yet believe, are blessed?

DISCUSSION PROMPT NO. 4: JOHN 20

Why does John think he has provided sufficient evidence for our belief in Jesus as the Messiah and Son of God? Do you agree or disagree? Why? What further evidence do you wish John would have included?

DISCUSSION PROMPT NO. 5: DEVOTIONAL REFLECTION

The writer notes, "The greater joy is ours who have become convinced beyond any need for proof." How does your belief in Christ affect your spiritual sight?

REFLECTIVE JOURNALING

_____

_____

_____

PSALM 2 ▪ EXODUS 14:21-31 ▪ 1 PETER 1:1-12 ▪ JOHN 14:1-17

MORNING MEDITATIONS

PRAYER—O God, Infinite Goodness, confirm your past mercies to me by enabling me for what remains of my life to be more faithful than I have been up until now to your great command to love as I have been loved. Let me not rest in any external devotion, nor trust in words or sighs or tears. Let me know and feel what it is to love you with all my heart. Amen. *JW*

PSALM 2:7-8—I will tell of the decree of the LORD: He said to me, "You are my son; today I have begotten you. Ask of me, and I will make the nations your heritage, and the ends of the earth your possession."

EXODUS 14:21b, 22a, 30a, 31b   *The People Feared the Lord*
The LORD drove the sea back by a strong east wind all night, and turned the sea into dry land . . . The Israelites went into the sea on dry ground . . . Thus the LORD saved Israel that day from the Egyptians . . . So the people feared the LORD and believed in the LORD and in his servant Moses.

1 PETER 1:3-4   *A Living Hope*
Blessed be the God and Father of our Lord Jesus Christ! By his great mercy he has given us a new birth into a living hope through the resurrection of Jesus Christ from the dead, and into an inheritance that is imperishable, undefiled, and unfading, kept in heaven for you.

JOHN 14:1-17   *Today's Gospel Reading*

The life that intends to be wholly obedient, wholly submissive, wholly listening, is astonishing in its completeness. Its joys are ravishing, its peace profound, its humility the deepest, its power world-shaking, its love enveloping, its simplicity that of a trusting child.
THOMAS R. KELLY, *A TESTAMENT OF DEVOTION*

EVENING REFLECTIONS

PSALM 7:10, 17—God is my shield, who saves the upright in heart . . . I will give to the LORD the thanks due to his righteousness, and sing praise to the name of the LORD, the Most High.

PRAYER—O God, deliver me from an idolatrous self-love. I know that this sin is the root of all evil. I praise you that in your infinite mercy you have granted me the grace to overcome it. I know you have made me, not to do my own will, but yours. Amen. *JW*

TUESDAY

PSALM 5 ▪ EXODUS 15:1-21 ▪ 1 PETER 1:13-25 ▪ JOHN 14:18-31

MORNING MEDITATIONS

PRAYER—Jesus, my Savior, let your love rule my heart without a rival. Let it dispose all my thoughts, words, and works; for then only can I fulfill my duty and your command of loving you with all my heart, and mind, and soul, and strength. Amen. **JW**

PSALM 5:3, 8a, 11a-b, 12—O Lord, in the morning you hear my voice; in the morning I plead my case to you, and watch . . . Lead me, O Lord, in your righteousness . . . Let all who take refuge in you rejoice; let them ever sing for joy . . . For you bless the righteous, O Lord; you cover them with favor as with a shield.

EXODUS 15:1b, 4a, 11, 13a *Who Is like You, O Lord?*
I will sing to the Lord, for he has triumphed gloriously . . . Pharaoh's chariots and his army he cast into the sea . . . Who is like you, O Lord, among the gods? Who is like you, majestic in holiness, awesome in splendor, doing wonders? . . . In your steadfast love you led the people whom you redeemed.

1 PETER 1:13, 15 *Prepare Your Minds for Action*
Therefore prepare your minds for action; discipline yourselves; set all your hope on the grace that Jesus Christ will bring you when he is revealed . . . As he who called you is holy, be holy yourselves in all your conduct.

JOHN 14:18-31 *Today's Gospel Reading*

> The life of obedience is a holy life, a separated life, a renounced life, cut off from worldly compromises, distinct, heaven-dedicated in the midst of others, stainless as the snows upon the mountain tops. THOMAS R. KELLY, *A TESTAMENT OF DEVOTION*

EVENING REFLECTIONS

PSALM 11:4, 7—The Lord is in his holy temple; the Lord's throne is in heaven. His eyes behold, his gaze examines humankind . . . The Lord is righteous; he loves righteous deeds; the upright shall behold his face.

PRAYER—O Lamb of God, be a guard to my desires so that I attach myself to nothing that will hinder an undivided love of you. O God, you have required of me that I love you with all my heart. Be both the assurance and the security of my heart's intention to be open to nothing except a complete love for you. Amen. **JW**

WEDNESDAY

PSALM 119:1-24 ▪ EXODUS 15:22—16:10 ▪ 1 PETER 2:1-25 ▪ JOHN 15:1-11

MORNING MEDITATIONS

PRAYER—Lord God, may I always honor your glorious name, and love the creation you have made. May your infinite goodness and greatness be adored by angels and humankind alike. May all who call themselves by your name catch a glimpse of that goodness. Amen. *JW*

PSALM 119:17-18—Deal bountifully with your servant, so that I may live and observe your word. Open my eyes, so that I may behold wondrous things out of your law.

EXODUS 15:26 *I Am the Lord Who Heals You*
He said, "If you will listen carefully to the voice of the LORD your God, and do what is right in his sight, and give heed to his commandments and keep all his statutes, I will not bring upon you any of the diseases that I brought upon the Egyptians; for I am the LORD who heals you."

1 PETER 2:24-25 *By His Wounds You Are Healed*
He himself bore our sins in his body on the cross, so that, free from sins, we might live for righteousness; by his wounds you have been healed. For you were going astray like sheep, but now you have returned to the shepherd and guardian of your souls.

JOHN 15:1-11 *Today's Gospel Reading*

Meister Eckhart wrote: "There are plenty to follow our Lord half-way, but not the other half. They will give up possessions, friends and honors, but it touches them too closely to disown themselves." It is just this astonishing life which is willing to follow him the other half . . . I propose to you.   THOMAS R. KELLY, *A TESTAMENT OF DEVOTION*

EVENING REFLECTIONS

PSALM 13:3, 5—Consider and answer me, O LORD my God! Give light to my eyes, or I will sleep the sleep of death . . . I trusted in your steadfast love; my heart shall rejoice in your salvation.

PRAYER—Merciful God, whatever you may deny me, do not deny me of your love. Save me from the idolatry of loving the world, or any of the things of the world. Take full possession of my heart, raise your throne in it, and rule there as you do in heaven. Amen. *JW*

PSALM 18:1-20 ▪ **EXODUS 16:10-21** ▪ **1 PETER 3:1-12** ▪ **JOHN 15:12-27**

MORNING MEDITATIONS

PRAYER—Eternal God, you have commanded me to renounce self. So give me strength, and I will obey your will. My choice, my desire is to love myself and others in and for you alone. May your mighty arm establish me, strengthen me, and settle me as both the foundation and pillar of my love. Amen. *JW*

PSALM 18:2-3—The LORD is my rock, my fortress, and my deliverer, my God, my rock in whom I take refuge, my shield . . . my stronghold. I call upon the LORD, who is worthy to be praised, so I shall be saved from my enemies.

EXODUS 16:14-15 *Bread from Heaven*
When the layer of dew lifted, there on the surface of the wilderness was a fine flaky substance, as fine as frost on the ground. When the Israelites saw it, they said to one another, "What is it?" . . . Moses said to them, "It is the bread that the LORD has given you to eat."

1 PETER 3:8, 9b *For This You Were Called*
Finally, all of you, have unity of spirit, sympathy, love for one another, a tender heart, and a humble mind . . . It is for this that you were called—that you might inherit a blessing.

JOHN 15:12-27 *Today's Gospel Reading*

He who walks in obedience, following God the second half, living the life of inner prayer, of submission and exultation, on him God's holiness takes hold as a mastering passion of life . . . Humility and holiness are twins in the astonishing birth of obedience in the hearts of people.
THOMAS R. KELLY, *A TESTAMENT OF DEVOTION*

EVENING REFLECTIONS

PSALM 18:31-32, 50a—For who is God except the LORD? And who is a rock besides our God?—the God who girded me with strength, and made my way safe . . . Great triumphs he gives to his king, and shows steadfast love to his anointed.

PRAYER—O my Father, my God, I ask you to deliver me from any passions that obstruct my knowledge and love of you. Let none of them find a way into my heart, but instead, give me a meek and gentle spirit. Reign in my heart; may I always be your servant and love you with all my heart. Amen. *JW*

PSALM 17 ▪ EXODUS 16:22-36 ▪ 1 PETER 3:13-4:6 ▪ JOHN 16:1-15

MORNING MEDITATIONS

PRAYER—O God, you are good and you do good. Your lovingkindness reaches everything you have made, but especially to us who are the work of your hand, made in your image with a capability of knowing and loving you eternally. May I not exclude anybody from my love today since they are the objects of your divine mercy, through Christ my Lord. Amen. *JW*

PSALM 17:6, 8, 15—I call upon you, for you will answer me, O God; incline your ear to me, hear my words . . . Guard me as the apple of [your] eye; hide me in the shadow of your wings . . . I shall behold your face in righteousness; when I awake I shall be satisfied, beholding your likeness.

EXODUS 16:31-32 *The Food I Fed You*
The house of Israel called it manna; it was like coriander seed, white, and the taste of it was like wafers made with honey. Moses said, "This is what the LORD has commanded: 'Let an omer of it be kept throughout your generations, in order that they may see the food with which I fed you in the wilderness.'"

1 PETER 3:15 *Sanctify Christ as Lord*
In your hearts sanctify Christ as Lord. Always be ready to make your defense to anyone who demands from you an accounting for the hope that is in you.

JOHN 16:1-15 *Today's Gospel Reading*

It must be understood that the Resurrection does not simply stand outside or above history. As something that breaks out of history and transcends it, the Resurrection nevertheless has its origins within history . . . Jesus' resurrection points beyond history but has left a footprint within it.   JOSEPH RATZINGER, *JESUS OF NAZARETH*

EVENING REFLECTIONS

PSALM 134:1-2—Come, bless the LORD, all you servants of the LORD, who stand by night in the house of the LORD! Lift up your hands in the holy place, and bless the LORD.

PRAYER—Father, let your love to me be the pattern of my love to my neighbor. You spared no expense to rescue me from the misery of my sinful past, so let me offer the benefit of the doubt to all those I know and love. May they, too, become your faithful servants, and may all Christians everywhere live up to the religion they profess. Amen. *JW*

PSALM 20 ▪ EXODUS 17:1-16 ▪ 1 PETER 4:7-19 ▪ JOHN 16:16-33

MORNING MEDITATIONS

PRAYER—Lord of life, you have destroyed death through the resurrection of your Son Jesus Christ. I pray today that I may live in his presence and rejoice in the hope of eternal glory. Amen.

PSALM 20:6-7—Now I know that the LORD will help his anointed; he will answer him from his holy heaven with might victories by his right hand. Some take pride in chariots, and some in horses, but our pride is in the name of the LORD our God.

EXODUS 17:5-6 *The Water I Gave You to Drink*
The LORD said to Moses, "Go on ahead of the people . . . take in your hand the staff with which you struck the Nile, and go. I will be standing there in front of you on the rock at Horeb. Strike the rock, and water will come out of it, so that the people may drink."

1 PETER 4:11 *May God Be Glorified in All Things*
Whoever speaks must do so as one speaking the very words of God; whoever serves must do so with the strength that God supplies, so that God may be glorified in all things through Jesus Christ. To him belong the glory and the power forever and ever. Amen.

JOHN 16:16-33 *Today's Gospel Reading*

Our Lord was trodden underfoot by death, and in turn trod upon death as upon a road. He submitted to death and endured it of his own free will, in order to destroy death against death's will . . . Death killed his natural life, but in its turn his supernatural life killed death.   ST. EPHRAEM, *SERMON ON OUR LORD*

EVENING REFLECTIONS

PSALM 116:1-2, 5—I love the LORD, because he has heard my voice and my supplications. Because he inclined his ear to me, therefore I will call on him as long as I live . . . Gracious is the LORD, and righteous; our God is merciful.

PRAYER—O God, forgive my enemies, and in due time make them my friends. Have mercy on all those who are afflicted in any way. Keep them patient in their sufferings. May we together take part in the joy of resurrection power through him who lives and reigns with you and the Holy Spirit, one God, world without end. Amen. *JW*

WEEK THREE

EASTER SEASON

Ashes to Fire Week 9

Sunday: Touch Me and See!

Read the Gospel passage from Luke 24:36b-48 and the devotional reflection titled "Touch Me and See!" then respond to the discussion prompts in the Reflective Journaling section.

THE MUSIC OF ASHES TO FIRE

Week 9: "Face to Face" (Track 10)

Monday through Saturday of Easter Season Week 3

IN THE MORNING:

A personal daily devotional guide includes prayer, a reading from the Old Testament, the Psalms, the Epistles, and the Gospel for each day of the week.

This week's readings are from Exodus, Colossians, and the Gospel of Matthew.

Inspirational quotes from men and women of faith keep us in contact with our shared Christian heritage.

IN THE EVENING:

An evening psalm and prayer become preludes to nighttime rest and renewal.

ẼASTER ṢEASON–WEEK THREE
Touch Me and See!

A devotional reflection based on Luke 24:36b-48

*R*ead the Gospel passage first, then the devotional reflection that follows. *The discussion prompts at the end will help prepare you for Sunday school and small-group sessions.*

Fear does strange things to us. Confronted by dangerous or mysterious events, even the most rational people can react in bizarre ways. The supernatural workings of God in our world sometimes cause people to run, faint, or cower in fear. That's why, throughout the Scriptures, we hear God and his angels repeating the words "Do not be afraid."

When Jesus was arrested in the garden of Gethsemane, the disciples ran like scared rabbits. We're told that Peter followed from a safe distance as the soldiers led Jesus to trial. When questioned by a servant girl, Peter swore he never knew the Lord. Fear causes us to do things that bring shame and regret.

On the third day after the crucifixion, no one was waiting for the resurrection. When the women went to visit the tomb, it was to anoint the dead body of Jesus with burial spices. But, Jesus had clearly told the disciples he would rise again. All his followers should have been camped out at the tomb entrance waiting for the stone to be rolled away. When Jesus walked out of the grave in triumph, a jubilant crowd should have been there to welcome him. *But no one was waiting for the resurrection.* The angels in heaven may have been singing the glory of God, but on earth, it was very quiet when the Father raised his Son from death.

Where were the disciples on the day of resurrection? John 20:19 tells us "the doors of the house where the disciples had met were locked for fear of the Jews." They were hiding, afraid that their lives were in danger because of their association with the crucified carpenter from Nazareth. What would happen next? They had no idea. But they were laying low until the danger passed.

And, suddenly, Jesus was . . . *there*! He didn't knock on the door or send a messenger; he just showed up, passing right through the locked doors. Now it was really time to be afraid! Luke 24:37 says, "They were startled and terrified." The human mind is not equipped for surprises like this. They had seen Jesus die; they knew where he was buried. But the person standing before them looked just like Jesus! Their desperate minds searched for answers and concluded they must be seeing a ghost.

Belief in ghosts is an amazingly persistent phenomenon throughout human history. A 2005 Gallup poll discovered that 32 percent of Americans believe in ghosts. In ancient cultures, such beliefs and superstitions were even more common. When Jesus walked on the water of the stormy Sea of Galilee, the disciples were sure they were seeing a ghost. And when the crucified Jesus appeared to them behind locked doors, they again suspected he was a ghost—the disembodied spirit of their master.

Jesus was anxious to assure them that he was not a ghost. He showed them the nail marks in his hands and feet. He said, "Touch me and see; for a ghost does not have flesh and bones as you see that I have" (v. 39). And then, to remove all doubt, he asked them for something to eat. Understandably, the disciples struggled to get their minds around the reality of a person who had died a bloody death and yet now stood in front of them eating a piece of fish.

So Jesus helped them draw out the life-changing implications of what they were witnessing. Everything the Scriptures had said about him was being fulfilled. Now that he had overcome death, it was time to start spreading the good news. They were to proclaim repentance and forgiveness of sins to all nations, beginning right there in the fear-filled city of Jerusalem.

When we picture this motley group of ordinary, uneducated men hunkered down behind locked doors in fear for their lives, it's hard to imagine they could ever begin to do what Jesus was commanding them. They were going to proclaim the gospel throughout the known world. Many of them would bravely face a martyr's death. The church would be built on the foundation of these apostles, with Christ Jesus himself as the chief cornerstone (Eph. 2:20). But let us remember that on the day Jesus rose from the dead, these men were hiding—afraid and defeated.

The disciples behind locked doors are like you and I when we let our fears determine our words and actions with regard to Jesus. Have I ever stayed quiet when an opportunity to share my faith was right in front of me? Have you perfected the art of finding excuses *not* to invite your neighbors into your home or to a gathering of your church family? Have we tried to eliminate all the risk and danger of discipleship?

The Bible doesn't try to cover up the embarrassing behavior of its main characters. If the Gospels had been written without the inspiration of the Holy Spirit, the authors surely would have tried to make the early church leaders look strong, brave, and heroic. The unpleasant details of fear, desertion, and denial could have been neatly edited out of the story. But the Gospels are the true story of God's triumph in spite of human sin and failure. "Where sin abounded, grace abounded much more" (Rom. 5:20, NKJV).

When the disciples saw and touched the body of their resurrected Lord, their fear was transformed into hope. Suddenly, they had a future again—they were commissioned to bear witness to Christ's triumph over death. And the resurrected Christ lives among us and in us today through the Holy Spirit. We have not only the testimony of eyewitnesses to the resurrection but also the Spirit of the Messiah, alive from the dead, living in us. Through the Spirit, the Lord whispers, "Do not be afraid." —RP

> ### After reading the passage from Luke 24:36b-48
> ### and the devotional reflection "Touch Me and See!"
> ### you may also want to read the following
> ### related passages:
> Acts 3:12-19; Psalm 4; and 1 John 3:1-7

The discussion prompts that follow will help prepare you to participate in your Sunday school class or small-group study. Use your Reflective Journaling section to record any other insights that come to you as you read the Gospel lesson and the devotional reflection.

DISCUSSION PROMPT NO. 1: LUKE 24

Why was it important that Jesus was physically resurrected and not a ghost?

DISCUSSION PROMPT NO. 2: LUKE 24

What is the significance of Jesus' resurrection for the disciples? What is the significance of the message the disciples were to preach?

DISCUSSION PROMPT NO. 3: LUKE 24

Think about Old Testament prophecies. How is Jesus the fulfillment of them? Why do you think it was important for Jesus to point that out?

DISCUSSION PROMPT NO. 4: LUKE 24

How did the disciples' experiences with Jesus equip them to be his witnesses? How does this truth inform our own ministry today?

DISCUSSION PROMPT NO. 5: DEVOTIONAL REFLECTION

How are the Gospels "the true story of God's triumph in spite of human sin and failure"? How is this statement true for you?

REFLECTIVE JOURNALING

_____

_____

_____

_____

_____

_____

_____

_____

_____

_____

_____

_____

_____

_____

_____

_____

_____

PSALM 25 ▪ **EXODUS 18:1-27** ▪ **1 PETER 5:1-14** ▪ **MATTHEW 3:1-6**

MORNING MEDITATIONS

PRAYER—Good Lord, pardon all my failures and make me today even more ardent and diligent in building up my soul in faith and love and obedience. Keep me aware of your presence all day long, and let your love fill and rule my soul in all those activities to which you call me today, in Jesus' name. Amen. *JW*

PSALM 25:1-2a, 4-5—To you, O LORD, I lift up my soul. O my God, in you I trust . . . Make me to know your ways, O LORD; teach me your paths. Lead me in your truth, and teach me, for you are the God of my salvation; for you I wait all day long.

EXODUS 18:8, 10-11a *The Lord Is Greater*

Then Moses told his father-in-law all that the LORD had done to Pharaoh and to the Egyptians for Israel's sake, all the hardship that had beset them on the way, and how the LORD had delivered them . . . Jethro said, "Blessed be the LORD, who has delivered you . . . Now I know that the LORD is greater than all gods."

1 PETER 5:7, 10b-11 *He Cares for You*

Cast all your anxiety on him, because he cares for you . . . the God of all grace, who has called you to his eternal glory in Christ, will himself restore, support, strengthen, and establish you. To him be the power forever and ever. Amen.

MATTHEW 3:1-6 *Today's Gospel Reading*

Christ is the only-begotten of God, to whom as to the Father we offer sacrifices; but by taking the form of a servant, Christ was made a priest through whom we can offer a living, holy sacrifice, pleasing to God. Nor could we have a sacrifice had not Christ become a victim for us; for in him the very nature of our race becomes a true and saving sacrifice.   ST. FULGENTIUS OF RUSPE, *LETTERS*

EVENING REFLECTIONS

PSALM 9:9-10—The LORD is a stronghold . . . in times of trouble. And those who know your name put their trust in you, for you, O LORD, have not forsaken those who seek you.

PRAYER—Shepherd of Israel, I ask you to embrace me tonight with your protection. Accept my poor service today, and pardon any sinfulness displayed in my behaviors or thoughts. I pray that you will conquer sin and misery, wherever it exists, in order to hasten your kingdom. Amen. *JW*

PSALM 26 ▪ EXODUS 19:1-16 ▪ COLOSSIANS 1:1-14 ▪ MATTHEW 3:7-12

MORNING MEDITATIONS

PRAYER—Lord, as I pass through this world, do not let my heart become its slave. Always fix my eyes, my undivided attention on the prize of my high calling. Prepare my heart for the joy that awaits those who love you and serve you. Amen. *JW*

PSALM 26:8, 12—O Lord, I love the house in which you dwell, and the place where your glory abides . . . My foot stands on level ground; in the great congregation I will bless the Lord.

EXODUS 19:3b, 4a-b *I Bore You on Eagles' Wings*
The Lord called to him from the mountain, saying . . . "You have seen what I did to the Egyptians, and how I bore you on eagles' wings and brought you to myself. Now therefore, if you obey my voice and keep my covenant, you shall be my treasured possession out of all the peoples.

COLOSSIANS 1:11-12a *Endure Everything with Patience*
May you be made strong with all the strength that comes from his glorious power, and may you be prepared to endure everything with patience, while joyfully giving thanks to the Father.

MATTHEW 3:7-12 *Today's Gospel Reading*

The Word of God is sacramental. That means it is sacred, and as a sacred word it makes present what it indicates . . . When we say God's word is sacred, we mean that God's word is full of God's presence. On the road to Emmaus, Jesus became present through his word.   HENRI J. M. NOUWEN, *WITH BURNING HEARTS*

EVENING REFLECTIONS

PSALM 39:7, 12a-b—And now, O Lord, what do I wait for? My hope is in you . . . Hear my prayer, O Lord, and give ear to my cry; do not hold your peace at my tears.

PRAYER—Lord, let me look upon the failings of my neighbors as if they were my own, that I may be grieved with them or for them, that I may never criticize them except as love requires it, and only then with tenderness and compassion. This I pray through Christ, my Lord. Amen. *JW*

PSALM 38 ▪ **EXODUS 20:1-21** ▪ **COLOSSIANS 1:15-23** ▪ **MATTHEW 3:13-17**

MORNING MEDITATIONS

PRAYER—Glory to you, O Jesus, who through the eternal Spirit offered yourself a full, perfect, and sufficient sacrifice for the sins of the whole world, rising the third day from the dead, and received all power both in heaven and earth. Hear my prayer. Amen. *JW*

PSALM 38:15, 21-22—It is for you, O LORD, that I wait; it is you, O Lord my God, who will answer . . . Do not forsake me, O LORD; O my God, do not be far from me; make haste to help me, O Lord, my salvation.

EXODUS 20:20-21   *Moses Drew Near to Where God Was*
Moses said to the people, "Do not be afraid; for God has come only to test you and to put the fear of him upon you so that you do not sin." Then the people stood at a distance, while Moses drew near to the thick darkness where God was.

COLOSSIANS 1:19-20   *God Was Pleased to Reconcile Us*
For in [Christ] all the fullness of God was pleased to dwell, and through him God was pleased to reconcile to himself all things, whether on earth or in heaven, by making peace through the blood of his cross.

MATTHEW 3:13-17   *Today's Gospel Reading*

The sacramental quality of the word makes God present not only as an intimate personal presence, but also as a presence that gives us a place in the great story of salvation. The God who becomes present to us . . . is the God . . . revealed to us in Jesus, the companion of our journey.   HENRI J. M. NOUWEN, *WITH BURNING HEARTS*

EVENING REFLECTIONS

PSALM 119:33-34, 41—Teach me, O LORD, the way of your statutes, and I will observe it to the end. Give me understanding, that I may keep your law and observe it with my whole heart . . . Let your steadfast love come to me, O LORD, your salvation according to your promise.

PRAYER—Father, bless all those who have been helpful to me throughout my life by their assistance, advice, and example. Bless all those who do not, or cannot pray for themselves. Change the hearts of my enemies and give me grace to forgive them, even as you for Christ's sake have forgiven them. Amen. *JW*

PSALM 37:1-18 ▪ EXODUS 23:10-33 ▪ COLOSSIANS 1:24—2:7 ▪ MATTHEW 4:1-11

MORNING MEDITATIONS

PRAYER—Father, I know that in love for me, being lost in sin, you sent your only Son, and that he, being the Lord of Glory, humbled himself to death upon the cross so that I might be raised to glory. Accept my thanks and praise. Amen. *JW*

PSALM 37:4-5, 7—Take delight in the LORD, and he will give you the desires of your heart. Commit your way to the LORD; trust in him, and he will act. Be still before the LORD, and wait patiently for him; do not fret over those who prosper in their way, over those who carry out evil devices.

EXODUS 23:20, 25   *You Shall Worship the Lord*
I am going to send an angel in front of you, to guard you on the way and to bring you to the place that I have prepared . . . You shall worship the LORD your God, and I will bless your bread and your water; and I will take sickness away from among you.

COLOSSIANS 2:6-7   *Live Your Lives in Christ*
As you therefore have received Christ Jesus the Lord, continue to live your lives in him, rooted and built up in him and established in the faith, just as you were taught, abounding in thanksgiving.

MATTHEW 4:1-11   *Today's Gospel Reading*

Without the word our life has little meaning, little vitality, and little energy. Without the word we remain little people with little concerns who live little lives and die little deaths . . . We need the word spoken and explained by the One who joins us on the road and makes his presence known to us—a presence first discerned in our burning hearts.

HENRI J. M. NOUWEN, *WITH BURNING HEARTS*

EVENING REFLECTIONS

PSALM 37:25, 27—I have been young, and now am old, yet I have not seen the righteous forsaken or their children begging bread . . . Depart from evil and do good; so you shall abide forever.

PRAYER—To you, O God, Father, Son and Holy Spirit, my Creator, Redeemer, and Sanctifier, I give up myself entirely; may I no longer serve myself, but you only, all the days of my life, through Christ my Lord, I pray. Amen. *JW*

FRIDAY

PSALM 105:1-22 ▪ EXODUS 24:1-18 ▪ COLOSSIANS 2:8-23 ▪
MATTHEW 4:12-17

MORNING MEDITATIONS

PRAYER—Almighty God, I bless you from my heart. O Savior of the World, God of God, Light of Light, you have destroyed the power of the devil, you have overcome death, and you sit at the right hand of the Father. Be today my light and peace, and make me a new creature, through Christ my Lord. Amen. **JW**

PSALM 105:1-3—O give thanks to the Lord, call on his name, make known his deeds among the peoples. Sing to him, sing praises to him; tell of all his wonderful works. Glory in his holy name; let the hearts of those who seek the Lord rejoice.

EXODUS 24:7 *We Will Be Obedient*
Then [Moses] took the book of the covenant, and read it in the hearing of the people; and they said, "All that the Lord has spoken we will do, and we will be obedient."

COLOSSIANS 2:13b-15 *He Forgave Us All Our Trespasses*
God made you alive together with him, when he forgave us all our trespasses, erasing the record that stood against us with its legal demands. He set this aside, nailing it to the cross. He disarmed the rulers and authorities and made a public example of them, triumphing over them in it.

MATTHEW 4:12-17 *Today's Gospel Reading*

The Creed is much more than a summary of the doctrine of the church. It is a profession of faith. And "faith," as the Greek word *pistis* shows, is an act of trust. It is the great "Yes" . . . It is this deep "Yes," not only to the words he spoke but also to him who spoke them, that brings us finally to His Table.   HENRI J. M. NOUWEN, *WITH BURNING HEARTS*

EVENING REFLECTIONS

PSALM 105:42-43, 45—He remembered his holy promise, and Abraham, his servant. So he brought his people out with joy, his chosen ones with singing . . . that they might keep his statutes and observe his laws. Praise the Lord!

PRAYER—O God, my Savior, my Sanctifier, keep your face turned toward me. Kindle within me the desires to confirm and increase my faith, and fulfill your plans for me. Amen. **JW**

PSALM 32 ▪ EXODUS 25:1-22 ▪ COLOSSIANS 3:1-17 ▪ MATTHEW 4:18-25

MORNING MEDITATIONS

PRAYER—Lord God, you have left us your holy word to be a lantern to our feet and a light unto our steps. Give us your Holy Spirit that out of the same word we may learn what your eternal will is and frame our lives in holy obedience to it, through Jesus Christ our Lord. Amen. *JW*

PSALM 32:1-2, 11—Happy are those whose transgression is forgiven, whose sin is covered. Happy are those to whom the LORD imputes no iniquity, and in whose spirit there is no deceit . . . Be glad in the LORD and rejoice, O righteous, and shout for joy, all you upright in heart.

EXODUS 25:1-2, 8 *Make Me a Sanctuary*
The LORD said to Moses: Tell the Israelites to take for me an offering; from all whose hearts prompt them to give you shall receive the offering for me . . . And have them make me a sanctuary, so that I may dwell among them.

COLOSSIANS 3:1, 3 *Raised with Christ*
So if you have been raised with Christ, seek the things that are above, where Christ is, seated at the right hand of God . . . for you have died, and your life is hidden with Christ in God.

MATTHEW 4:18-25 *Today's Gospel Reading*

Communion with Jesus means becoming like him. With him we are nailed on the cross, with him we are laid in the tomb, with him we are raised up . . . It ushers us into the Kingdom. There we belong to Christ and Christ to us, and with Christ we belong to God.

HENRI J. M. NOUWEN, *WITH BURNING HEARTS*

EVENING REFLECTIONS

PSALM 42:1-2a, 8—As a deer longs for flowing streams, so my soul longs for you, O God. My soul thirsts for God, for the living God . . . By day the LORD commands his steadfast love; and at night his song is with me, a prayer to the God of my life.

PRAYER—O God, be gracious to all who are near and dear to me. You know their names and their needs. In your goodness, bless them according to those needs through Jesus Christ my Lord. Amen. *JW*

WEEK FOUR
*E*ASTER *S*EASON

Ashes to Fire Week 10

Sunday: I AM, the Good Shepherd

Read the Gospel passage from John 10:11-18 and the devotional reflection titled "I AM, the Good Shepherd," then respond to the discussion prompts in the Reflective Journaling section.

THE MUSIC OF ASHES TO FIRE

Week 10: "All Hail the Power of Jesus' Name" (Track 11)

Monday through Saturday of Easter Season Week 4

IN THE MORNING:

A personal daily devotional guide includes prayer, a reading from the Old Testament, the Psalms, the Epistles, and the Gospel for each day of the week.

This week's readings are from Exodus, I Thessalonians, and the Gospel of Matthew.

Inspirational quotes from men and women of faith keep us in contact with our shared Christian heritage.

IN THE EVENING:

An evening psalm and prayer become preludes to nighttime rest and renewal.

EASTER SEASON—WEEK FOUR
I AM, the Good Shepherd

A devotional reflection based on John 10:11-18

*R*ead the Gospel passage first, then the devotional reflection that follows. *The discussion prompts at the end will help prepare you for Sunday school and small-group sessions.*

As we drove around the countryside of England that day, flocks of sheep were scampering around pastures as we passed. To me, all the sheep looked pretty much the same except that they bore a specific colored marking on their wool that proclaimed, "We belong to this flock." There was something intimate and intensely personal in the scene that reminded me of Jesus' statement, "I am the good shepherd" (John 10:11a).

The Scriptures affirm that the same Lord who was present at creation is the One who took on human form and entered into our existence by teaching, loving, suffering, and dying for us. Today, on this fourth Sunday of Easter, we consider the One who incarnates those qualities, the One who clothes himself with the rich imagery of the Good Shepherd who lovingly cares for his sheep.

The familiar Shepherd Psalm (Ps. 23) is a good place to begin. By announcing that the Lord is *my* shepherd, the psalmist answers an important question. To which flock do we belong? Who owns us? In our modern society, many might view this image negatively, as something oppressive or restrictive. "I'm self-made, I'm my own person. No one owns me," our contemporaries declare. Yet what or who we set our sights on tends to determine the contours of our lives.

So what difference might it make for us as followers of Christ when we let the reality of this relationship with the Good Shepherd sink deeply into the core of who we are? Just as the sheep bore the mark of the shepherd to distinguish the flock's owner, so we, too, bear the mark of Christ in our lives. How will those around us know we are the sheep of his pasture, the flock under his care?

The mark of a Christian, Jesus reminds us, is love. Jesus Christ laid down his life for us. He didn't just *say* he loved us. Jesus demonstrated his love actively, purposefully, meaningfully, and redemptively. As the Good Shepherd, he says, "I lay down my life for the sheep" (John 10:15b). Later, in the upper room with his disciples he would say, "No one has greater love than this, to lay down one's life for one's friends" (15:13). Here is a challenge to all who want to be known by his name. We also ought to find ways to love actively and deeply, even to the laying down of our lives for our brothers and sisters. One question we can ask is in what ways, both big and small, can we find opportunities to extend ourselves to others in love every day?

Jesus calls us to be *fully* in the flock. We should let these questions guide us: How can we say how much we love God and yet ignore, or walk by, brothers and sisters in need? Is it sometimes true that we are one person at church where we espouse love for others, and another person at work where we behave just the opposite? When sheep on the other side of the fence look over into our pasture, what do they see? Does our flock bear the mark of our Good Shepherd?

While it is true that Jesus has modeled for us a love that finds expression in words and in actions, it is not our actions that earn us a place in the Shepherd's flock. It is liberating to know that what we do *for* God comes from hearts seeking to respond *to* God's love—not hoping to *win* God's love. We want to follow the example of the Good Shepherd, not because the act in and of itself earns God's love, but because we are responding to God's unconditional love by living authentically with his mark.

How does the shepherd care for the flock? The shepherd has a deep knowledge of the needs of the sheep. He knows their need for water, rest, and food. He is always aware about possible dangers. The imagery of the twenty-third psalm depicts a shepherd who intimately knows the ways of his sheep, the vagaries of the land, and the prey and lovingly promises his presence.

The Lord is *our* Shepherd. The Lord is present as a constant companion. There are situations in our lives that deprive us of our balance and threaten to rob us of our joy. At times we can become cast down when the burden is heavy. Yet Christ the Good Shepherd is there to pick us up and bring us back to safety. When depression darkens our souls, we can feel the touch of Christ's eternal joy, which, unlike fleeting happiness, finds its source more profoundly in the experience of Christ's presence.

Are there areas where we need to feel the Good Shepherd's touch to restore our souls? In those times, we can see our return to health as a partnership of the gracious work of Christ's restoring love with the healing resources we have around us. Beyond that, we have the support and strength of the community of faith holding us up both in prayer and in tangible support.

Who is *our* Shepherd? It is the Lord who shepherds us; it is God, in Christ, who leads us. "Surely goodness and love will follow me all the days of my life," the psalmist wrote (Ps. 23:6*a*, NIV). One way of looking at this promise is to recognize that goodness, love, and mercy will follow us in every situation of life. We do not have the assurance that we will not experience pain and suffering but that Christ's presence brings goodness, love, and mercy and the awareness that God's love will not let us go. "And I will dwell in the house of the Lord forever" (v. 6*b*, NIV). —JL

> ### After reading the passage from John 10:11-18 and
> ### the devotional reflection "I AM, the Good Shepherd,"
> ### you may also want to read the following
> ### related passages:
> Acts 4:5-12; Psalm 23; 1 John 3:16-24

The discussion prompts that follow will help prepare you to participate in your Sunday school class or small-group study. Use your Reflective Journaling section to record any other insights that come to you as you read the Gospel lesson and the devotional reflection.

DISCUSSION PROMPT NO. 1: DEVOTIONAL REFLECTION

The writer notes that while we are not exempt from suffering and pain, we can be assured of the Lord's goodness and mercy following us, or pursuing us, in all of life's situations. How have you experienced the goodness and mercy of the Good Shepherd?

DISCUSSION PROMPT NO. 2: JOHN 10

Sheep and shepherds have been a dominant metaphor for the relationships of the church with Jesus and within the church as the community of faith. What else can you say about how these images describe Jesus and us beyond what is said in this particular passage?

DISCUSSION PROMPT NO. 3: JOHN 10

Who is the wolf in this analogy? Who are the hired hands? Who are the sheep? How does this analogy help you understand your spiritual life?

DISCUSSION PROMPT NO. 4: JOHN 10

According to verses 14-15, what is the relationship between the sheep and the shepherd?

DISCUSSION PROMPT NO. 5: JOHN 10

Why do you think it was important to Jesus to make it clear that he lays down his life voluntarily, that it is not taken by force?

REFLECTIVE JOURNALING

_____

_____

_____

_____

_____

_____

_____

_____

_____

_____

_____

_____

_____

_____

_____

_____

_____

_____

PSALM 52 ▪ EXODUS 31:12-18 ▪ COLOSSIANS 3:18—4:6 (7-18) ▪ MATTHEW 5:1-10

MORNING MEDITATIONS

PRAYER—O God, you are the giver of all good gifts and I desire to praise your name for all of your goodness to me. I thank you for sending your Son to die for my sins, for the means of grace, and for the hope of glory, through Jesus Christ. Amen. **JW**

PSALM 52:8b-9—I trust in the steadfast love of God forever and ever. I will thank you forever, because of what you have done. In the presence of the faithful I will proclaim your name, for it is good.

EXODUS 31:12-13 *I, the Lord, Sanctify You*
The LORD said to Moses: You yourself are to speak to the Israelites: "You shall keep my sabbaths, for this is a sign between me and you throughout your generations, given in order that you may know that I, the LORD, sanctify you."

COLOSSIANS 4:5-6 *Gracious Speech*
Conduct yourselves wisely toward outsiders, making the most of the time. Let your speech always be gracious, seasoned with salt, so that you may know how you ought to answer everyone.

MATTHEW 5:1-10 *Today's Gospel Reading*

It is as if [Jesus] had said straight out, "The proof that I know the Father and the Father knows me is the fact that I lay down my life for my sheep; that is to say, the love which leads me to die for my sheep shows how much I love the Father."

ST. GREGORY THE GREAT, FROM A HOMILY

EVENING REFLECTIONS

PSALM 44:1, 4a, 5—We have heard with our ears, O God, our ancestors have told us, what deeds you performed in their days, in the days of old . . . You are my King and my God . . . through you we push down our foes; through your name we tread down our assailants.

PRAYER—Lord Christ, I do not ask you for the things of this world; give them to whomever you please. I only desire your mercy. Save me, O God; accept my imperfect repentance, and receive me into your care and keeping. Amen. **JW**

**PSALM 45 ▪ EXODUS 32:1-34 ▪ 1 THESSALONIANS 1:1-10 ▪
MATTHEW 5:11-16**

MORNING MEDITATIONS

PRAYER—Lord Jesus, give me the mind that is in you. Let me learn to be meek and lowly and pour into me the whole spirit of divine humility. Fill every part of my soul with it, and make it the ruling habit of both mind and heart. Amen. *JW*

PSALM 45:6-7a—Your throne, O God, endures forever and ever. Your royal scepter is a scepter of equity; you love righteousness and hate wickedness.

EXODUS 32:30-31 *If You Will Only Forgive Their Sin*
Moses said to the people, ". . . I will go up to the LORD; perhaps I can make atonement for your sin." So Moses returned to the LORD and said, "Alas, this people has sinned a great sin; they have made for themselves gods of gold. But now, if you will only forgive their sin—but if not, blot me out of the book that you have written."

1 THESSALONIANS 1:7, 9-10 *You Turned to God from Idols*
You became an example to all the believers . . . For the people of those regions report . . . how you turned to God from idols, to serve a living and true God, and to wait for his Son from heaven, whom he raised from the dead—Jesus, who rescues us from the wrath that is coming.

MATTHEW 5:11-16 *Today's Gospel Reading*

Man desires to praise you. He is but a tiny part of all that you have created. He bears about him his mortality . . . yet this tiny part of all that you have created desires to praise you . . . For you have made us for yourself and our hearts are restless till they rest in you.

ST. AUGUSTINE, *CONFESSIONS*

EVENING REFLECTIONS

PSALM 48:1, 9-10a—Great is the LORD and greatly to be praised in the city of our God . . . We ponder your steadfast love, O God, in the midst of your temple. Your name, O God, like your praise, reaches to the ends of the earth.

PRAYER—O Lamb of God, give me grace throughout my whole life, in every thought, and word and work, to imitate your meekness and humility. May I go through all the scenes of life not seeking my own glory, but looking wholly unto you, and acting wholly for you, through Christ my Lord. Amen. *JW*

PSALM 119:49-72 ▪ **EXODUS 33:1-23** ▪ **1 THESSALONIANS 2:1-12** ▪ **MATTHEW 5:17-20**

MORNING MEDITATIONS

PRAYER—Lord God, send your Holy Spirit to be the guide of all my ways and the sanctifier of my soul and body. Give me the light of your presence, your peace from heaven, and the salvation of my soul, through Jesus Christ my Lord. Amen. **JW**

PSALM 119:57-58—The LORD is my portion; I promise to keep your words. I implore your favor with all my heart; be gracious to me according to your promise.

EXODUS 33:19, 21-22   *I Will Cover You with My Hand*
And [God] said, "I will make all my goodness pass before you, and will proclaim before you the name, 'The LORD' . . . And the LORD continued, "See, there is a place by me where you shall stand on the rock; and while my glory passes by I will put you in a cleft of the rock, and I will cover you with my hand."

1 THESSALONIANS 2:11-12   *Lead a Life Worthy of God*
As you know, we dealt with each one of you like a father with his children, urging and encouraging you and pleading that you lead a life worthy of God, who calls you into his own kingdom and glory.

MATTHEW 5:17-20   *Today's Gospel Reading*

The God of love is willing to save all the souls that he has made. This he has proclaimed to them in his Word, together with the terms of salvation, revealed by the Son of his love, who gave his own life that they who believe in him might have everlasting life.

JOHN WESLEY, *THE WEDDING GARMENT* (A SERMON)

EVENING REFLECTIONS

PSALM 49:3, 7, 15a—My mouth shall speak wisdom; the meditation of my heart shall be understanding . . . Truly, no ransom avails for one's life, there is no price one can give to God for it . . . God will ransom my soul.

PRAYER—Father, grant me forgiveness of what is past, that in the days to come I may with a pure spirit, do your will—walking humbly with you, showing love to all, and keeping body and soul in sanctification and honor, in Jesus' name. Amen. **JW**

PSALM 50 ▪ EXODUS 34:1-17 ▪ 1 THESSALONIANS 2:13-20 ▪ MATTHEW 5:21-26

MORNING MEDITATIONS

PRAYER—Eternal God, my Sovereign Lord, I acknowledge all I am, all I have is yours. I humbly thank you for all the blessings you have bestowed upon me—for creating me in your own image, for redeeming me by the death of your blessed Son, and for the assistance of the Holy Spirit, through Christ I pray. Amen. **JW**

PSALM 50:14, 23—Offer to God a sacrifice of thanksgiving, and pay your vows to the Most High . . .Those who bring thanksgiving as their sacrifice honor me; to those who go the right way I will show the salvation of God.

EXODUS 34:6-7a-b   *A God Merciful and Gracious*
The LORD passed before him, and proclaimed, "The LORD, the LORD, a God merciful and gracious, slow to anger, and abounding in steadfast love and faithfulness, keeping steadfast love for the thousandth generation, forgiving iniquity and transgression and sin."

1 THESSALONIANS 2:13   *God's Word Is at Work in You*
We also constantly give thanks to God for this, that when you received the word of God that you heard from us, you accepted it not as a human word but as what it really is, God's word, which is also at work in you believers.

MATTHEW 5:21-26   *Today's Gospel Reading*

Throughout this time between the Lord's resurrection and ascension, the Lord in his providence fulfilled one purpose, taught one lesson, set one consideration before the eyes and hearts of his followers: that the Lord Jesus Christ, who was truly born, truly suffered and truly died, should be recognized as truly risen. ST. LEO THE GREAT, *SERMON ONE—ASCENSION*

EVENING REFLECTIONS

PSALM 115:1, 18—Not to us, O LORD, not to us, but to your name give glory, for the sake of your steadfast love and your faithfulness . . . We will bless the LORD from this time on and forevermore. Praise the LORD!

PRAYER—O my God, I love you above all things, with my whole heart and soul, because you are worthy of all my love. I forgive all who have injured me, and I ask pardon for all whom I may have injured. Amen. **JW**

**PSALM 54 ▪ EXODUS 34:18-35 ▪ 1 THESSALONIANS 3:1-13 ▪
MATTHEW 5:27-37**

MORNING MEDITATIONS

PRAYER—Almighty God, I bless you from my heart. O Savior of the World, God of God, Light of Light, you have destroyed the power of the devil, you have overcome death, and you sit at the right hand of the Father. Be today my light and peace and make me a new creature, through Christ my Lord. Amen. **JW**

PSALM 54:2, 4, 6—Hear my prayer, O God; give ear to the words of my mouth . . . Surely, God is my helper; the Lord is the upholder of my life . . . With a freewill offering I will sacrifice to you; I will give thanks to your name, O LORD, for it is good.

EXODUS 34:29   *Moses' Face Shone*
Moses came down from Mount Sinai. As he came down from the mountain with the two tablets of the covenant in his hand, Moses did not know that the skin of his face shone because he had been talking with God.

1 THESSALONIANS 3:11-13   *May He Strengthen Your Heart in Holiness*
Now may our God and Father himself and our Lord Jesus Christ . . . make you increase and abound in love for one another and for all . . . And may he so strengthen your hearts in holiness that you may be blameless before our God and Father at the coming of our Lord Jesus with all his saints.

MATTHEW 5:27-37   *Today's Gospel Reading*

We make our sacrifice of prayer in spirit . . . This is the offering which he has asked for. This is the sacrifice, offered from the heart, fed on faith, prepared by truth, unblemished in innocence, pure in chastity, garlanded with love, which we must bring to God's altar.

TERTULLIAN, *TREATISE ON PRAYER*

EVENING REFLECTIONS

PSALM 51:15-16a, 17—O Lord, open my lips, and my mouth will declare your praise. For you have no delight in sacrifice . . . The sacrifice acceptable to God is a broken spirit; a broken and contrite heart, O God, you will not despise.

PRAYER—Father, accept my imperfect repentance, . . . forgive my faults, purify my motives, strengthen my weakness, and let your good Spirit watch over me, and your love ever rule my heart, through the mercies of Jesus, I pray. Amen. **JW**

PSALM 55 ▪ **EXODUS 40:18-38** ▪ **1 THESSALONIANS 4:1-12** ▪
MATTHEW 5:38-48

MORNING MEDITATIONS

PRAYER—Preserve me, O God, from all those snares and temptations which continually draw my attention away from you. Guide me by your Holy Spirit in all those places where your providence will lead me today. May none of my experiences make me inattentive to your presence or lukewarm in your service. Amen. **JW**

PSALM 55:16-18a—But I call upon God, and the LORD will save me. Evening and morning and at noon I utter my complaint and moan, and he will hear my voice. He will redeem me unharmed from the battle that I wage.

EXODUS 40:18a, 33-34 *Moses Finished the Work*
Moses set up the tabernacle . . . He set up the court around the tabernacle and the altar, and put up the screen at the gate of the court. So Moses finished the work. Then the cloud covered the tent of meeting, and the glory of the LORD filled the tabernacle.

1 THESSALONIANS 4:1, 3a *Your Sanctification Is God's Will*
Finally, brothers and sisters, we ask and urge you in the Lord Jesus that, as you learned from us how you ought to live and to please God . . . you should do so more and more . . . For this is the will of God, your sanctification.

MATTHEW 5:38-48 *Today's Gospel Reading*

Because Christ wished to show his disciples how necessary it is to be rooted in love of him . . . he told them in figurative language that he was the vine, and that the branches of the vine were those who were united with him . . . By the gift of the Spirit they are united with him by faith and every kind of holiness.

ST. CYRIL OF ALEXANDRIA, *COMMENTARY ON JOHN'S GOSPEL*

EVENING REFLECTIONS

PSALM 139:1, 17-18—O LORD, you have searched me and known me . . . How weighty to me are your thoughts, O God! How vast is the sum of them! I try to count them—they are more than the sand; I come to the end—I am still with you.

PRAYER—O God, your kingdom rules over all. Rule in the hearts of your people, but especially in my heart. Forgive my enemies, and give them repentance and charity, and grant me grace always to overcome evil with good. Amen. **JW**

WEEK FIVE

EASTER SEASON

Ashes to Fire Week 11

Sunday: I AM, the Vine

Read the Gospel passage from John 15:1-8 and the devotional reflection titled "I AM, the Vine," then respond to the discussion prompts in the Reflective Journaling section.

THE MUSIC OF ASHES TO FIRE

Week 11: "Your Throne" (Track 12)

Monday through Saturday of Easter Season Week 5

IN THE MORNING:

A personal daily devotional guide includes prayer, a reading from the Old Testament, the Psalms, the Epistles, and the Gospel for each day of the week.

This week's readings are from Leviticus, 1 and 2 Thessalonians, and the Gospel of Matthew.

Inspirational quotes from men and women of faith keep us in contact with our shared Christian heritage.

IN THE EVENING:

An evening psalm and prayer become preludes to nighttime rest and renewal.

EASTER SEASON—WEEK FIVE
I AM, the Vine

A devotional reflection based on John 15:1-8

*R**ead the Gospel passage first, then the devotional reflection that follows. The discussion prompts at the end will help prepare you for Sunday school and small-group sessions.*

A woman in our town recently opened a small restaurant, which in itself is not newsworthy. The story behind her new venture deserves attention. Prior to opening her restaurant, she operated a bar and liquor store in town. She earned a comfortable income from them. She couldn't put her finger on it, but the pieces of the puzzle of her life weren't fitting together as she wanted. She experienced an increasing level of discontent with both her life and way of making a living. This discontent led her into a deep soul-searching. She slowly came to recognize God's hand reaching out to her. In her words, "I was not searching for him; he came searching for me and found me." She began reading the Bible and soon confessed Jesus as Savior and Lord of her life.

With Jesus as her Lord, she knew she had to close the bar and liquor store. But what would she do to make a living? She was a single mother with a child to feed and care for. She had always wanted to operate a restaurant, so she stepped out on faith and focused all of her energy on bringing this dream to reality. The restaurant quickly became one of the most popular places in town. She serves delicious food. If you want to have one of her meals, you'd better come early. Lines form quickly. And you'd better be prepared to hear how Jesus sought and found her. She loves to tell everyone about his seeking love.

Jesus paints a picture with vines, branches, fruit, and a gardener in John 15:1-8. He employs images from Psalm 80. Contemporary readers often read this passage and conclude, "Jesus says I need to work harder at producing good fruit for God." Wrong! Jesus' imagery points not so much to me as a branch and the fruit I must produce as it points to Jesus the true Vine and the Father as Gardener. The Vine and the Gardener nurture and produce fruit in me.

The Easter season reminds us of the incredible love of our heavenly Father. His love sought us and reached out to us. His love sacrificed his only Son to die on the cross for the forgiveness of our sins. His love raised Jesus from the dead as a validation of his life, message, and ministry to the world. His love accepted us as his children and welcomed us into the family of God. In another place, John captures the evidence of God's love for us: "This is how God showed his love among us: He sent his one and only Son into the world that we might live through him. This is love: not that we loved God, but that he loved us and sent his Son as an atoning sacrifice for our sins" (1 John 4:9-10, NIV).

I think of this John 15 imagery every time I look out the sunroom window at my next-door neighbor tending his flower garden. He is a master gardener with a yard filled with flowers in every color of the rainbow. He tends his garden from early morning until sundown just about every day of the week. He works hard on his knees, loves his flowers, and nurtures them to their height of productivity. I can't look at his beautiful flowers without thinking about all of the love and hard work that go into their development. That's what John relates in this passage of Scripture. It's not about us and our fruit; it's about God's great love to us and his incredible sacrifice for us.

Easter reminds us of the unique message of the Christian faith. So often our religiously pluralistic world urges us to give equal status to all of the religions of the world. "All paths lead to the same God," we're told. Not so. Christian faith takes an opposite approach from every other religion in the world. World religions focus on our efforts at reaching out to God through acts of worship, devotion, and sacrifice. Christian faith reminds us that God first reached out to us and drew us to himself. He showed us his great love by sending his Son as a sacrifice for our sins.

God reached out to our local bar and liquor store operator. He found her, invited her, changed her, and gave her eternal life. What he did for her he wants to do for everyone who will recognize his voice and accept his invitation. What an amazing picture of the tireless Gardner tending his garden and producing beautiful results. All he asks of us is to abide in Jesus, the true Vine, and let him work through us. That's the fruit of living the Easter message. —FM

After reading the passage from John 15:1-8 and the devotional reflection "I AM, the Vine," you may also want to read the following related passages:

Acts 8:26-40; Psalm 22:25-31; 1 John 4:7-21

The discussion prompts that follow will help prepare you to participate in your Sunday school class or small-group study. Use your Reflective Journaling section to record any other insights that come to you as you read the Gospel lesson and the devotional reflection.

DISCUSSION PROMPT NO. 1: JOHN 15

Why does the vine grower prune the vine? What does this mean for us today?

DISCUSSION PROMPT NO. 2: JOHN 15

What might be the fruit Jesus is talking about? What is the purpose of this fruit?

DISCUSSION PROMPT NO. 3: JOHN 15

Just as a branch cannot bear fruit on its own, a Christian cannot bear spiritual fruit apart from Christ. Why?

DISCUSSION PROMPT NO. 4: JOHN 15

Jesus invites those who abide in him to ask him for whatever they wish. What would you like to ask him for today? How is your desire an expression of Christ's words abiding in you?

DISCUSSION PROMPT NO. 5: JOHN 15

Do you find these words of Jesus comforting? Explain.

DISCUSSION PROMPT NO. 6: DEVOTIONAL REFLECTION

How does the personal experience of the devotional writer in "I AM, the Vine" help you with your own understanding of this passage?

Reflective Journaling

_____

_____

_____

PSALM 57 ▪ LEVITICUS 16:1-19 ▪ 1 THESSALONIANS 4:13-18 ▪ MATTHEW 6:1-6, 16-18

MORNING MEDITATIONS

PRAYER—O God, you have blessed me with your love and the provisions of life. For health and strength, for food and clothing, for everything necessary to my existence, I offer you my profound thanks and praise. Amen. **JW**

PSALM 57:2-3a, 3c—I cry to God Most High, to God who fulfills his purpose for me. He will send from heaven and save me . . . God will send forth his steadfast love and his faithfulness.

LEVITICUS 16:6a, 18a, 19   He Shall Make Atonement
Aaron shall offer the bull as a sin offering for himself . . . Then [Aaron] shall go out to the altar that is before the LORD and make atonement on [Israel's] behalf . . . [and] shall sprinkle some of the blood on it with his finger seven times, and cleanse it and hallow it from the uncleanness of the people of Israel.

1 THESSALONIANS 4:14, 16   The Dead in Christ Will Rise First
For since we believe that Jesus died and rose again, even so, through Jesus, God will bring with him those who have died . . . For the Lord himself, with a cry of command, with the archangel's call and with the sound of God's trumpet, will descend from heaven, and the dead in Christ will rise first.

MATTHEW 6:1-6, 16-18   Today's Gospel Reading

This is why [Jesus] warned people to "count the cost" before becoming Christians. "Make no mistake," he says, "if you let me, I will make you perfect. The moment you put yourself into my hands, that is what you are in for. Nothing less, or other, than that."

C. S. LEWIS, *MERE CHRISTIANITY*

EVENING REFLECTIONS

PSALM 64:10—Let the righteous rejoice in the LORD and take refuge in him. Let all the upright in heart glory.

PRAYER—Gracious Holy Spirit, look with mercy on all those who suffer affliction. Hear the cries of the sick, the oppressed, the imprisoned, the poor and needy. Give to my enemies grace and pardon. Enable me to love them, to bless those who curse me, to do good to those who despise me, and to pray for those who mistreat me. Amen. **JW**

**PSALM 62 ▪ LEVITICUS 16:20-34 ▪ 1 THESSALONIANS 5:1-11 ▪
MATTHEW 6:7-15**

MORNING MEDITATIONS

PRAYER—O eternal Father, in your mercy accept my thanksgiving for bringing me to another day. For this day, and every day of my life, I ask that all my thoughts, words and works will bring glory to you. Heal my infirmities, strengthen my weaknesses, and forgive all my sins, in Jesus' name. Amen. *JW*

PSALM 62:1-2, 11-12a—For God alone my soul waits in silence; from him comes my salvation. He alone is my rock and my salvation, my fortress; I shall never be shaken . . . Once God has spoken; twice I have heard this: that power belongs to God, and steadfast love belongs to you, O Lord.

LEVITICUS 16:30-31   *You Shall Be Clean Before the Lord*
For on this day atonement shall be made for you, to cleanse you; from all your sins you shall be clean before the LORD. It is a sabbath of complete rest to you, and you shall deny yourselves; it is a statute forever.

1 THESSALONIANS 5:9-10   *Our Destiny Is Salvation*
For God has destined us not for wrath but for obtaining salvation through our Lord Jesus Christ, who died for us, so that whether we are awake or asleep we may live with him.

MATTHEW 6:7-15   *Today's Gospel Reading*

You have free will, and if you choose, you can push me away. But if you do not push me away, understand that I am going to see this job through. Whatever suffering it may cost you in your earthly life . . . whatever it costs me, I will never rest, nor let you rest, until you are literally perfect—until my Father can say without reservation that he is well pleased with you.   C. S. LEWIS, *MERE CHRISTIANITY*

EVENING REFLECTIONS

PSALM 68:4, 35—Sing to God, sing praises to his name; lift up a song to him who rides upon the clouds—his name is the LORD—be exultant before him . . . Awesome is God in his sanctuary, the God of Israel; he gives power and strength to his people. Blessed be God!

PRAYER—O God, create in me a zealous obedience to all your commands, a cheerful patience under all circumstances, and a thankful heart for all your blessings. May I be constantly thinking of you, and blessing your name with thoughts of joyful adoration. Amen. *JW*

WEDNESDAY

**PSALM 72 ▪ LEVITICUS 19:1-18 ▪ 1 THESSALONIANS 5:12-28 ▪
MATTHEW 6:19-24**

MORNING MEDITATIONS

PRAYER—Lord and Savior, you are the way, the truth and the life. You have said that we cannot follow you unless we renounce ourselves. I know, my Savior, that you place no requirement upon us that we cannot bear with the assistance of your grace. May I seek only your will in all things. Amen. *JW*

PSALM 72:18-19—Blessed be the Lord, the God of Israel, who alone does wondrous things. Blessed be his glorious name forever; may his glory fill the whole earth. Amen and Amen.

LEVITICUS 19:1-2 *You Shall Be Holy*
The Lord spoke to Moses, saying: Speak to all the congregation of the people of Israel and say to them: You shall be holy, for I the Lord your God am holy.

1 THESSALONIANS 5:23-24 *May God Sanctify You Entirely*
May the God of peace himself sanctify you entirely; and may your spirit and soul and body be kept sound and blameless at the coming of our Lord Jesus Christ. The one who calls you is faithful, and he will do this.

MATTHEW 6:19-24 *Today's Gospel Reading*

On one hand, God's demand for perfection need not discourage you in the least . . . He knows perfectly well that your own efforts are never going to bring you anywhere near perfection. On the other hand, you must realize from the outset that the goal toward which he is beginning to guide you is absolute perfection. That is what you are in for.

C. S. LEWIS, *MERE CHRISTIANITY*

EVENING REFLECTIONS

PSALM 119:76-77—Let your steadfast love become my comfort according to your promise to your servant. Let your mercy come to me, that I may live; for your law is my delight.

PRAYER—O Lord my Redeemer and my Judge, where I have failed, be my advocate. Spare me, gracious Savior, and let your mercy be magnified in me. Deliver me from the power of sin, and preserve me in your mercy. Amen. *JW*

PSALM 70 ▪ LEVITICUS 19:26-37 ▪ 2 THESSALONIANS 1:1-12 ▪ MATTHEW 6:25-34

MORNING MEDITATIONS

PRAYER—Eternal God, my Sovereign Lord, watch over me today with eyes of mercy, direct my soul and body according to your will, and fill my heart with your Holy Spirit that I may live this day, and all the rest of my days, to your glory. Amen. *JW*

PSALM 70:4-5—Let all who seek you rejoice and be glad in you. Let those who love your salvation say evermore, "God is great!" But I am poor and needy; hasten to me, O God! You are my help and my deliverer; O Lord, do not delay!

LEVITICUS 19:33, 34b *You Shall Love the Alien*
When an alien resides with you in your land, you shall not oppress the alien . . . you shall love the alien as yourself, for you were aliens in the land of Egypt: I am the Lord your God.

2 THESSALONIANS 1:11-12a *God Make You Worthy of His Call*
[We are] asking that our God will make you worthy of his call and will fulfill by his power every good resolve and work of faith, so that the name of our Lord Jesus may be glorified in you.

MATTHEW 6:25-34 *Today's Gospel Reading*

The Christian way is different: harder, and easier. Christ says, "Give me All. I don't want so much of your time and so much of your money and so much of your work. I want *you*. I have not come to torment your natural self, but to kill it."   C. S. LEWIS, *MERE CHRISTIANITY*

EVENING REFLECTIONS

PSALM 74:12, 16—Yet God my King is from of old, working salvation in the earth . . . Yours is the day, yours also the night; you established the luminaries and the sun.

PRAYER—Father, you have instructed me with your laws, and enlightened me with your statutes. You have redeemed me by the blood of your Son and sanctified me by the grace of your Holy Spirit. For these and all your other mercies, in love I seek to honor your great name as I rest in your love. Amen. *JW*

PSALM 106:1-18 ▪ LEVITICUS 23:1-22 ▪ 2 THESSALONIANS 2:1-17 ▪ MATTHEW 7:1-12

MORNING MEDITATIONS

PRAYER—In your mercy, O God, accept my morning sacrifice of praise and thanksgiving. I offer it up to you with a full heart. You are praised by all your works. Amidst the jubilation of nature, do not let your human family remain silent. Let those of us who are your children offer the noblest praise. Amen. *JW*

PSALM 106:4, 5b-c—Remember me, O Lord, when you show favor to your people; help me when you deliver them . . . that I may rejoice in the gladness of your nation, that I may glory in your heritage.

LEVITICUS 23:1-2a, 3   *A Sabbath to the Lord*
The Lord spoke to Moses, saying, Speak to the people of Israel and say to them . . . Six days shall work be done; but the seventh day is a sabbath of complete rest, a holy convocation; you shall do no work; it is a sabbath to the Lord.

2 THESSALONIANS 2:13   *Salvation Through Sanctification by the Spirit*
But we must always give thanks to God for you, brothers and sisters beloved by the Lord, because God chose you as the first fruits for salvation through sanctification by the Spirit and through belief in the truth.

MATTHEW 7:1-12   *Today's Gospel Reading*

[Christ says], "No half measures are any good. I don't want to cut off a branch here and a branch there, I want to have the whole tree down . . . Hand over the whole natural self, all the desires which you think innocent as well as the ones you think wicked. . . I will give you a new self instead. In fact, I will give you Myself—my own will shall become yours."

C. S. LEWIS, *MERE CHRISTIANITY*

EVENING REFLECTIONS

PSALM 106:47-48—Save us, O Lord our God, and gather us from among the nations, that we may give thanks to your holy name and glory in your praise. Blessed be the Lord, the God of Israel, from everlasting to everlasting. And let all the people say, "Amen."

PRAYER—O Lord Jesus, I give you my body, my soul, my substance, my fame, my liberty, my life. I am not mine, but yours. I ask you to contend for me when I am assaulted, heal me when I am wounded, and revive me when I am brought low. Amen. *JW*

PSALM 76 ▪ LEVITICUS 23:23-44 ▪ 2 THESSALONIANS 3:1-18 ▪ MATTHEW 7:13-21

MORNING MEDITATIONS

PRAYER—Savior and Sanctifier of my soul, put your grace in my heart so that I may honor you today with worship in spirit and truth. You have made me and sent me into the world to do your work. Now assist me to fulfill the purpose for which I was born by giving myself gladly to your service. Amen. **JW**

PSALM 76:7-9—But you indeed are awesome! Who can stand before you . . . From the heavens you uttered judgment; the earth feared and was still when God rose up to establish judgment, to save all the oppressed of the earth.

LEVITICUS 23:26-27, 28b   *A Day of Atonement on Your Behalf*
The LORD spoke to Moses, saying: Now, the tenth day of this seventh month is the day of atonement; it shall be a holy convocation for you: you shall deny yourselves and present the Lord's offering by fire . . . it is a day of atonement . . . on your behalf before the LORD your God.

2 THESSALONIANS 3:4-5   *We Have Confidence in the Lord*
And we have confidence in the Lord concerning you, that you are doing and will go on doing the things that we command. May the Lord direct your hearts to the love of God and to the steadfastness of Christ.

MATTHEW 7:13-21   *Today's Gospel Reading*

When he clothed himself in human nature, Christ received this glory, which he had from all ages, before the world existed; and when his human nature was thus glorified by the Holy Spirit, the glory of the Spirit could be handed on to Christ's family, beginning with his disciples.   ST. GREGORY OF NYSSA, *HOMILY 15*

EVENING REFLECTIONS

PSALM 27:13-14—I believe that I shall see the goodness of the LORD in the land of the living. Wait for the LORD; be strong, and let your heart take courage; wait for the LORD!

PRAYER—My Father, have compassion on any and all who are distressed in mind, body, or spirit. Give them, and grant to me, your grace, a steady patience, and timely deliverance in the hour of need, through Christ I pray. Amen. **JW**

WEEK SIX

EASTER SEASON

Ashes to Fire Week 12

Sunday: You Are My Friends

Read the Gospel passage from John 15:9-17 and the devotional reflection titled "You Are My Friends," then respond to the discussion prompts in the Reflective Journaling section.

THE MUSIC OF ASHES TO FIRE

Week 12: "Come Let Us Sing unto the Lord" (Track 13)

Monday through Saturday of Easter Season Week 6

IN THE MORNING:

A personal daily devotional guide includes prayer, a reading from the Old Testament, the Psalms, the Epistles, and the Gospel for each day of the week.

This week's readings are from Leviticus, Daniel, 1 Samuel, 2 Kings, Numbers, Colossians, 1 Timothy, Revelation, Ephesians, and the Gospel of Matthew.

Inspirational quotes from men and women of faith keep us in contact with our shared Christian heritage.

IN THE EVENING:

An evening psalm and prayer become preludes to nighttime rest and renewal.

EASTER SEASON–WEEK SIX
You Are My Friends

A devotional reflection based on John 15:9-17

*R*ead the Gospel passage first, then the devotional reflection that follows. The discussion prompts at the end will help prepare you for Sunday school and small-group sessions.

One of the greatest joys of parenting occurs when children imitate their parents. It doesn't matter what they imitate; they're always cute. We're amused at the picture of a little girl imitating her mother baking cookies or a little boy mowing the lawn like his father. Parents enjoy the compliment of their children's imitation. That joy multiplies one hundred times when parents see their grown children pass their values and practices on to their grandchildren. Family habits, traditions, and values flow freely and naturally from loving relationships between family members. Imitation is seldom planned; it just happens through the give-and-take of daily life.

What is true of normal family interactions is also true of Christian interactions. Christians share their own set of values and practices. Where do you suppose Christians get their highly treasured values and practices? From imitating the loving relationship that exists between the Father, Son, and Holy Spirit. Our loving relationships flow naturally from imitating the way the members of the Trinity relate to one another. Our imitation gives us another clue that God made us in his image and for fellowship with himself. We love one another the way the heavenly Father, the Son, and the Spirit love each other.

Prior to Jesus coming in the flesh to join us in our world, we humans knew nothing about this loving relationship between Father, Son, and Spirit. We had many puzzle pieces from Old Testament readings, but we couldn't put the pieces together to make a clear picture. Jesus changed all of that by telling us plainly about this incredible love bond that exists within the Trinity.

One of the most amazing revelations of Jesus' earthly teachings is that we don't have to stand on the outside and look through a window at this love relationship between the Father, Son, and Spirit. Jesus extends his hand and invites us to join them, to become part of God's family, and to share in their love for one another. We don't have to create this love from within ourselves; we receive it as a gift from God. It comes with our adoption into his family. It comes not as a one-time deposit but as a daily flow into our hearts and lives. It comes freely to us; we pass it on freely to everyone we meet and live with.

Jesus makes another startling revelation in this passage, a revelation offered by none of the other religions of the world. Jesus tells us we can be a friend of God and have a daily relationship with him. What a daring claim! I can become a friend of the Almighty Sovereign of the universe. Knowledge of God remained shrouded in mystery and darkness from ages past, but no longer. Jesus turns the light on and reveals the truth about God to us. God loves us as his children. He wants a daily, loving relationship with us. We are friends of God. Amazing!

Jesus talks here, for the first time in his earthly ministry, about his joy. Imagine that. Jesus speaks to his disciples in the shadow of the cross about his great joy. He is about to go willingly into battle with sin, Satan, and death. Yet he senses joy welling up within him. It just might be that he already begins to feel the victory over this battle he is heading into. He must walk the way of the cross, but the Father has already assured him of certain victory. Jesus proved by his example that we can experience God's love and joy in the midst of adversity, trial, and difficult circumstances. The book of Hebrews give us a brief glimpse into this thought when it says, "Looking to Jesus the pioneer and perfecter of our faith, who for the sake of the joy that was set before him endured the cross, disregarding its shame, and has taken his seat at the right hand of the throne of God" (12:2).

Jesus wants us to share not only in his love but also in his joy. Like love, we do not produce our own joy. We receive it as a gift from God. God's joy comes to us as a benefit of our daily relationship with him. How much joy does Jesus offer in John 15:11? Not just a little joy now and then but a heart filled with joy always!

Jesus indicates that one of the ways we evidence love for God is by loving one another. This includes loving fellow Christians as well as those we regard as enemies. None of us have the self-generated ability to love fully in this manner. We must receive this love as a gift from God. Again, freely received, freely given.

Just as the line from the chorus says, "They'll know we are Christians by our love."

Divine love, divine joy, friend of God. All gifts of an Easter faith. —FM

After reading the passage from John 15:9-17 and the devotional reflection "You Are My Friends," you may also want to read the following related passages:
Acts 10:44-48; Psalm 98; and 1 John 5:1-6

The discussion prompts that follow will help prepare you to participate in your Sunday school class or small-group study. Use your Reflective Journaling section to record any other insights that come to you as you read the Gospel lesson and the devotional reflection.

DISCUSSION PROMPT NO. 1: JOHN 15

How does obedience to Jesus keep us abiding in his love? Why are obedience and love inseparable aspects of the Christian life?

DISCUSSION PROMPT NO. 2: JOHN 15

How does obeying Jesus bring joy into our lives? Give examples.

DISCUSSION PROMPT NO. 3: JOHN 15

Why do you think Jesus commanded us to love our fellow Christians? What role do you think this plays in our wider ministry to the world?

DISCUSSION PROMPT NO. 4: JOHN 15

Jesus put verse 13 into practice by dying on the cross. What are some ways we can lay our lives down for one another today?

DISCUSSION PROMPT NO. 5: DEVOTIONAL REFLECTION

What is the "great joy" Jesus wants to share with his friends?

REFLECTIVE JOURNALING

_____

_____

_____

_____

PSALM 80 ▪ LEVITICUS 25:35-55 ▪ COLOSSIANS 1:9-14 ▪ MATTHEW 13:1-16

MORNING MEDITATIONS

PRAYER—O God, you are the giver of all good gifts and I desire to praise your name for all of your goodness to me. I thank you for sending your Son to die for my sins, for the means of grace, and for the hope of glory, through Jesus Christ. Amen. **JW**

PSALM 80:1, 2b—Give ear, O Shepherd of Israel, you who lead Joseph like a flock! You who are enthroned upon the cherubim, shine forth . . . Stir up your might, and come to save us!

LEVITICUS 25:55   *I Brought You Out of Egypt*
For to me the people of Israel are servants; they are my servants whom I brought out from the land of Egypt: I am the Lord your God.

COLOSSIANS 1:11b-12a, 13-14   *He Has Rescued Us*
May you be prepared to endure everything with patience, while joyfully giving thanks to the Father, who . . . has rescued us from the power of darkness and transferred us into the kingdom of his beloved Son, in whom we have redemption, the forgiveness of sins.

MATTHEW 13:1-16   *Today's Gospel Reading*

Because Christ is living I can have certain knowledge. It doesn't take deep intellect and profound philosophy to grasp the fact of the Resurrection—only a loving heart. The women saw first, and told. And love has been seeing Him ever since.

BERTHA MUNRO, *TRUTH FOR TODAY*

EVENING REFLECTIONS

PSALM 77:11-14a—I will call to mind the deeds of the Lord; I will remember your wonders of old. I will meditate on all your work, and muse on your might deeds. Your way, O God, is holy. What god is so great as our God? You are the God who works wonders.

PRAYER—O God, I give you my affections: my love, my fear, my joy. What you love may I love. What displeases you, may it displease me. I give you my body. May I glorify you with it, and preserve it holy, fit for you to dwell in. May I neither indulge it, nor abuse it, but keep it healthy, vigorous, and active and fit to serve you with all my heart. Amen. **JW**

PSALM 78:1-39 ▪ LEVITICUS 26:1-20 ▪ 1 TIMOTHY 2:1-6 ▪ MATTHEW 13:18-23

MORNING MEDITATIONS

PRAYER—O God my Savior and Sanctifier, give me the mind that is in you. Let me learn to be meek and lowly, and pour into me the whole spirit of divine humility. Fill every part of my soul with it, and make it the ruling habit of both mind and heart. Amen. *JW*

PSALM 78:5-7a—He established a decree in Jacob . . . which he commanded our ancestors to teach to their children; that the next generation might know them, the children yet unborn, and rise up and tell them to their children, so that they should set their hope in God.

LEVITICUS 26:11-13a *I Will Walk Among You*
I will place my dwelling in your midst, and I shall not abhor you. And I will walk among you, and will be your God, and you shall be my people. I am the LORD your God who brought you out of the land of Egypt.

1 TIMOTHY 2:3b-6a *There Is One Mediator*
God our Savior . . . desires everyone to be saved and to come to the knowledge of the truth. For there is one God; there is also one mediator between God and humankind, Christ Jesus, himself human, who gave himself a ransom for all.

MATTHEW 13:18-23 *Today's Gospel Reading*

It was wonderful to have Jesus with them in flesh and blood . . . But they were to learn that although the body they had loved was gone, a far more glorious Christ was theirs forever. They were to learn that the spiritual always excels the material, that when God takes away one blessing he always gives a better. Have we learned these things?

BERTHA MUNRO, *TRUTH FOR TODAY*

EVENING REFLECTIONS

PSALM 78:52-53a, 54a—Then he led out his people like sheep, and guided them in the wilderness like a flock. He led them in safety, so that they were not afraid . . . and he brought them to his holy hill.

PRAYER—O God, your Son was despised and rejected. When I am slighted by my friends, or disdained by my superiors, or ridiculed by my equals, then I will simply pray, "It is now that I begin to be a disciple of Christ." Amen. *JW*

WEDNESDAY

**PSALM 119:97-120 • 2 KINGS 2:1-15 • EPHESIANS 1:1-10 •
MATTHEW 22:41-46**

MORNING MEDITATIONS

PRAYER—Lord God, . . . [a]ccept my thanks for keeping me through the night, and may I be wholly devoted to your service today. Send your Holy Spirit to be my guide, the sanctifier of my soul and body. Save, defend and build me up in your fear and love. Amen. **JW**

PSALM 119:105, 111—Your word is a lamp to my feet and a light to my path . . . Your decrees are my heritage forever; they are the joy of my heart.

2 KINGS 2:9b-10a-b, 11   *Let Me Inherit a Double Share of Your Spirit*
Elisha said, "Please let me inherit a double share of your spirit." [Elijah] responded, ". . . If you see me as I am being taken from you, it will be granted" . . . As they continued walking and talking, a chariot of fire and horses separated the two of them, and Elijah ascended in a whirlwind into heaven.

EPHESIANS 1:3, 9-10a   *Blessed with Every Spiritual Blessing*
Blessed be the God and Father of our Lord Jesus Christ, who has blessed us in Christ with every spiritual blessing in the heavenly places . . . [and] has made known to us the mystery of his will, according to his good pleasure that he set forth in Christ, as a plan for the fullness of time, to gather up all things in him.

MATTHEW 22:41-46   *Today's Gospel Reading*

Because Christ is living I can have unwavering faith . . . Faith can die . . . Even the hope that "springs eternal in the human breast" must yield to stubborn facts. But the Christian's hope faces every ugly fact and still is triumphant. It is founded on the Resurrection.

BERTHA MUNRO, *TRUTH FOR TODAY*

EVENING REFLECTIONS

PSALM 68:1a, 4—Let God rise up, let his enemies be scattered . . . Sing to God, sing praises to his name; lift up a song to him who rides upon the clouds—his name is the LORD—be exultant before him.

PRAYER—My Lord and my God, I know that unless I am planted together with you in the likeness of your death that I cannot share in your resurrection. Strengthen me, that by denying myself and taking up my cross daily, I may crucify all that is not like you, and utterly destroy all sin. Amen. **JW**

PSALM 47 ▪ DANIEL 7:9-14 ▪ REVELATION 5:1-14 ▪ MATTHEW 28:16-20

MORNING MEDITATIONS

PRAYER—Lord Jesus, help me with your grace so that whatever I do and experience today it may bring glory to you. Increase my love for you and for all people. Direct my paths and teach me to keep you always before me. Amen. **JW**

PSALM 47:5-7—God has gone up with a shout, the LORD with the sound of the trumpet. Sing praises to God, sing praises; sing praises to our King, sing praises. For God is king of all the earth; sing praises with a psalm.

DANIEL 7:9-10b   *The Ancient One Took His Throne*
As I watched, thrones were set in place, and an Ancient One took his throne, his clothing was white as snow, and the hair of his head like pure wool; his throne was fiery flames . . . a thousand thousands served him, and ten thousand times ten thousand stood attending him.

REVELATION 5:5b, 13b   *Worthy Is the Lamb*
"Do not weep. See, the Lion of the tribe of Judah, the Root of David, has conquered" . . . "To the one seated on the throne and to the Lamb be blessing and honor and glory and might forever and ever!"

MATTHEW 28:16-20   *Today's Gospel Reading*

Take Jesus out of your life, and what have you? Emptiness. But you never need lose him now. It was better that he went, because he ascended with all power and he sent the Spirit with omnipresence. A walk with Jesus—what a privilege. But [for the disciples] it had to end. My privilege is rarer: he abides with me, goes out with me when I must go, returns when I return.   BERTHA MUNRO, *TRUTH FOR TODAY*

EVENING REFLECTIONS

PSALM 96:7, 9-10a—Ascribe to the LORD, O families of the peoples, ascribe to the LORD glory and strength . . . Worship the LORD in holy splendor; tremble before him, all the earth. Say among the nations, "The LORD is king!"

PRAYER—O God, Father, Son and Holy Spirit, I give you all my worldly goods. May I prize them and use them only for you. I will restore them to you by sharing them with the poor, and will be content to part with them whenever you ask them from me. Amen. **JW**

PSALM 86 ▪ 1 SAMUEL 2:1-10 ▪ EPHESIANS 2:1-10 ▪ MATTHEW 7:22-27

MORNING MEDITATIONS

PRAYER—O God, I give you my understanding. May it be my first concern to know you, your perfection, your works and your will. Silence any reasonings that conflict with what you teach me. I give you my will; may it always submit to yours. May I will your glory in all things; delighting to do your will and rejoicing in it. Amen. *JW*

PSALM 86:4-5, 8—Gladden the soul of your servant, for to you, O Lord, I lift up my soul. For you, O Lord, are good and forgiving, abounding in steadfast love to all who call on you . . . There is none like you among the gods, O Lord, nor are there any works like yours.

1 SAMUEL 2:2, 10b   *There Is No Rock like Our God*
There is no Holy One like the Lord, no one besides you; there is no Rock like our God . . . The Lord will judge the ends of the earth; he will give strength to his king, and exalt the power of his anointed.

EPHESIANS 2:4a, 5b-6   *Seated in Heavenly Places*
But God . . . made us alive together with Christ—by grace you have been saved—and raised us up with him and seated us with him in the heavenly places in Christ Jesus.

MATTHEW 7:22-27   *Today's Gospel Reading*

Jesus is not dead. He is not a Name only, not a historic Fact only, not a beautiful Life only, not a removed, distant Atonement only. He is living: He is Person; High Priest, and through the Spirit is Companion, Friend, Counselor, Great Lover . . . That living fellowship has implications I must realize—or he is as good as dead to me.

BERTHA MUNRO, *TRUTH FOR TODAY*

EVENING REFLECTIONS

PSALM 92:1-2, 4—It is good to give thanks to the Lord, to sing praises to your name, O Most High; to declare your steadfast love in the morning, and your faithfulness by night . . . For you, O Lord, have made me glad by your work; at the works of your hands I sing for joy.

PRAYER—O God the Father, have mercy on me. O God the Son, who knowing the will of the Father, came into the world to save me, have mercy on me. O God the Holy Spirit who has breathed holy thoughts in me, have mercy on me. Holy Trinity, I adore you as One God. Have mercy on me. Amen. *JW*

**PSALM 90 ▪ NUMBERS 11:16-17, 24-29 ▪ EPHESIANS 2:11-22 ▪
MATTHEW 7:28—8:4**

MORNING MEDITATIONS

PRAYER—O God, put your grace into my heart so I may praise your great and glorious name. You have made me, and you send me into the world to do your work. Assist me to fulfill the purpose of my creation, and to show my praise by giving myself to your service. Amen. **JW**

PSALM 90:1-2—Lord, you have been our dwelling place in all generations. Before the mountains were brought forth, or ever you had formed the earth and the world, from everlasting to everlasting you are God.

NUMBERS 11:25, 29 *The Spirit of the Lord*
Then the Lord came down . . . and took some of the spirit that was on him [Moses] and put it on the seventy elders; and when the spirit rested upon them, they prophesied . . . Moses said to him, ". . . Would that all the Lord's people were prophets, and that the Lord would put his spirit on them!"

EPHESIANS 2:17-18 *Access in One Spirit*
So he came and proclaimed peace to you who were far off and peace to those who were near; for through him both of us have access in one Spirit to the Father.

MATTHEW 7:28—8:4 *Today's Gospel Reading*

Jesus with us as a Person means power. Through the abiding Holy Spirit his presence is made real, and we are made positive Christians . . . In the war against sin the Spirit gives power to witness and to intercede; and that conquering Presence carries the fight into the enemy's territory.   BERTHA MUNRO, *TRUTH FOR TODAY*

EVENING REFLECTIONS

PSALM 136:23-24, 26—It is he who remembered us in our low estate, for his steadfast love endures forever; and rescued us from our foes, for his steadfast love endures forever . . . O give thanks to the God of heaven, for his steadfast love endures forever.

PRAYER—O Father of mercy, accept my humble thanks for your watchful care today. Continue to show me your lovingkindness, and protect me through the night. Let your holy angels watch over me and defend me. Let me rest in peace and rise with eagerness to serve you. Amen. **JW**

WEEK SEVEN

EASTER SEASON

Ashes to Fire Week 13

Sunday: A Holy Church

Read the Gospel passage from John 17:6-19 and the devotional reflection titled "A Holy Church," then respond to the discussion prompts in the Reflective Journaling section.

THE MUSIC OF ASHES TO FIRE

Week 13: "Alleluia, Christ Is Risen" (Track 14)

Monday through Saturday of Easter Season Week 7

IN THE MORNING:

A personal daily devotional guide includes prayer, a reading from the Old Testament, the Psalms, the Epistles, and the Gospel for each day of the week.

This week's readings include passages from Joshua, I Samuel; the prophets Isaiah, Zechariah, Jeremiah, and Ezekiel; and Ephesians and the Gospel of Matthew

Inspirational quotes from men and women of faith keep us in contact with our shared Christian heritage.

IN THE EVENING:

An evening psalm and prayer become preludes to nighttime rest and renewal.

ℰASTER ℐEASON–WEEK SEVEN
A Holy Church

A devotional reflection based on John 17:6-19

*R*ead the Gospel passage first, then the devotional reflection that follows. The discussion prompts at the end will help prepare you for Sunday school and small-group sessions.

Much of my childhood was spent on the front pew of the Church of the Nazarene in a little lumber town in Western Oregon. My front-pew location was not an indication of my piety. It was simply the place where my parents could keep a watchful eye on me from the choir. From my first-row vantage point I often witnessed my parents leading worship in various ways. Dad led the singing. Mom was our local mission society president.

One of the vivid memories of those years is my parents singing a duet, a gospel song that was popular in those days titled "On the Jericho Road." Part of the chorus says:

> On the Jericho Road there's room for just two.
> No more and no less, just Jesus and you.

I loved hearing my parents sing that song, but it never dawned on me as a young boy that it was strange not only for that song to be presented as a duet but also that the whole idea of "room for just two" didn't fit with New Testament discipleship. It is fair to say that at least part of the reason the error of that idea never dawned on me was that it never dawned on anybody who taught me the Christian way.

My family and the congregation that nurtured my mind and heart in the life of Jesus taught me that the supreme concern was my personal relationship with Jesus Christ. Of course, there is nothing wrong with that. I am deeply grateful to have learned that one can indeed enjoy a personal relationship with God through Jesus Christ. I have since discovered, however, that Christian life is at the heart a community life. I would now say that my supreme concern is not only for my personal relationship with Jesus Christ but also that I might live as a true Christian within the community of faith so that our life together begins to show the world what the kingdom of God is like.

Could it be that the *holiness* to which we are committed has as much to do with how *we* act and live together as it does with how *you* act and live individually? There is no doubt that the grace of God's sanctifying work is thoroughly personal. A life marked by the very character and spirit of Jesus is personal, but it is not private. This truth is clear throughout the Scriptures, and it is beautifully evident in the way Jesus prays for us just before he goes to the cross.

The wonderful prayer of Jesus in John 17 has the balance just right. Jesus does begin by praying for himself. His relationship with the Father is personal. It is not private, however, for Jesus quickly moves in his prayer to the relationship that the triune God desires with all who would believe. Jesus' prayer for us is a corporate prayer, and as he prays for us together, one of the main things he prays for is that we would be holy.

Jesus prays for us, "Sanctify them by the truth" (v. 17, NIV). His longing is that in our life together we might experience what it means to be a sanctified church. What does this mean? It means we are set apart; we are given a new identity and mission. It means we no longer live by the values and priorities of this world. So he prays, "They are not of the world any more than I am of the world" (v. 14, NIV). And yet by his sanctifying grace we are to live in this world as his distinctive people. Jesus says, "My prayer is not that you take them out of the world but that you protect them from the evil one" (v. 15, NIV).

Jesus imagines more than a collection of holy individuals that happen to get together on Sundays. He imagines a holy church where the result is greater than the sum of the parts. Something powerful and new happens as God's people join together to impact this world as a people who by the very quality of their lives together and their love for each other make an eternal mark on the world and point people to a God of love and grace.

So Jesus prays, "I sanctify myself [I set myself apart for a holy purpose)], that they [we, us] too may be truly sanctified [set apart for a holy purpose]" (v. 19, NIV). Everywhere the New Testament places the idea of a sanctified discipleship squarely within the context of the community of faith. Even as Jesus continues his prayer he says, "May they . . . be one as we are one" (vv. 21-22, NIV).

So how are we doing? Are we the kind of church where the Spirit of Christ can move, work, cleanse, and transform so that somehow in our corporate life we become an answer to Jesus' prayer? Are we remembering that our worship is not about our personal preferences but about the exaltation of Christ and the praise of God's glorious grace? Are we remembering that the gospel will never allow us to remain in broken relationships with each other? Is forgiveness active among us?

Are we remembering that we can only be a holy church when we live in unity together, preferring one another above ourselves and laying aside petty differences for the greater mission? Are we remembering that our whole reason to exist has to do with those who are not yet a part of us?

Jesus prayed for us that we would be holy. He died and rose again to make us holy. He is working even now to make us holy. Let us be careful never to resist the work of Christ in our midst. Let's always be responsive and open, living in surrender to the Lordship of Christ, not only individually but also together.

Truth is, on the Jericho road there is room for more than just two. There is room for all who join the company of the redeemed and commit to walking together on this wonderful highway of holiness. —JR

After reading the passage from John 17:6-19 and the devotional reflection "A Holy Church," you may also want to read the following related passages:

Acts 1:15-17, 21-26; Psalm 1; 1 John 5:9-13

The discussion prompts that follow will help prepare you to participate in your Sunday school class or small-group study. Use your Reflective Journaling section to record any other insights that come to you as you read the Gospel lesson and the devotional reflection.

DISCUSSION PROMPT NO. 1: JOHN 17

Explain what it means to be "in the world" but "not of the world." Why is this an important way for Christians to live?

DISCUSSION PROMPT NO. 2: JOHN 17

How do Jesus' words in this passage make his joy complete in us (see also John 15:9-24)? How does this fit with the idea that the world will hate us?

DISCUSSION PROMPT NO. 3: JOHN 17

Jesus prayed for the disciples' protection in, not removal from, the world. Why did Jesus pray this way?

DISCUSSION PROMPT NO. 4: JOHN 17

What does it mean to be sanctified by the truth of God's Word? What are the implications for contemporary Christians?

DISCUSSION PROMPT NO. 5: DEVOTIONAL REFLECTION

Comment on the writer's question: "Are we remembering that the gospel will never allow us to remain in broken relationships with each other?" What does it say to the church? What does it mean for you?

REFLECTIVE JOURNALING

_____

_____

_____

_____

_____

_____

_____

_____

_____

_____

_____

_____

_____

_____

_____

_____

PSALM 89:1-18 ▪ JOSHUA 1:1-9 ▪ EPHESIANS 3:1-13 ▪ MATTHEW 8:5-17

MORNING MEDITATIONS

PRAYER—O God, you are the giver of all good gifts and I desire to praise your name for all of your goodness to me. I thank you for sending your Son to die for my sins, for the means of grace, and for the hope of glory, through Jesus Christ. Amen. *JW*

PSALM 89:1-2—I will sing of your steadfast love, O LORD, forever; with my mouth I will proclaim your faithfulness to all generations. I declare that your steadfast love is established forever; your faithfulness is as firm as the heavens.

JOSHUA 1:8a, 9 *Be Strong and Courageous*
This book of the law shall not depart out of your mouth; you shall meditate on it day and night, so that you may be careful to act in accordance with all that is written in it . . . Be strong and courageous; do not be frightened or dismayed, for the LORD your God is with you wherever you go.

EPHESIANS 3:8b, 10a, 11-12 *We Have Access to God in Boldness*
This grace was given to me to bring to the Gentiles the news of the boundless riches of Christ . . . so that through the church the wisdom of God in its rich variety might now be made known . . . This was in accordance with the eternal purpose that he has carried out in Christ Jesus our Lord, in whom we have access to God in boldness and confidence through faith in him.

MATTHEW 8:5-17 *Today's Gospel Reading*

The thought is full of unspeakable glory—that God the Holy Spirit can come into my heart and fill it so full that the life of God will manifest itself all through this body which used to manifest just the opposite.   OSWALD CHAMBERS, *BIBLICAL PSYCHOLOGY*

EVENING REFLECTIONS

PSALM 89:19a, 24, 28a—Then you spoke in a vision to your faithful one, and said . . . "My faithfulness and steadfast love shall be with him; and in my name his horn shall be exalted . . . Forever I will keep my steadfast love for him.

PRAYER—O God, let your unwearied and tender love to me make my love unwearied and tender toward my neighbors, always fervent in my prayers for their health, safety, ease, and happiness. Make me peaceful, easy to forgive, and glad to return good for evil. Amen. *JW*

PSALM 99 ▪ 1 SAMUEL 16:1-13a ▪ EPHESIANS 3:14-21 ▪ MATTHEW 8:18-27

MORNING MEDITATIONS

PRAYER—My Lord and my God, you see my heart; and my desires are not hidden from you. I am encouraged and strengthened by your goodness to me today. I want to be yours and yours alone, O God, my Savior, my Sanctifier. Hear me, help me, show mercy to me for Jesus Christ's sake. Amen. *JW*

PSALM 99:1, 5—The LORD is king; let the peoples tremble! He sits enthroned upon the cherubim; let the earth quake! . . . Extol the LORD our God; worship at his footstool. Holy is he!

1 SAMUEL 16:12c-13a   *This Is the One*
The LORD said, "Rise and anoint him; for this is the one." Then Samuel took the horn of oil, and anointed him in the presence of his brothers; and the spirit of the LORD came mightily upon David from that day forward.

EPHESIANS 3:16-17a   *May Christ Dwell in Your Hearts by Faith*
I pray that, according to the riches of his glory, he may grant that you may be strengthened in your inner being with power through his Spirit, and that Christ may dwell in your hearts through faith.

MATTHEW 8:18-27   *Today's Gospel Reading*

Christ's atoning death and the inner working of the Holy Spirit have power to cleanse the heart of the believer to its innermost depths and bring the believer to the place where Christ is the supreme and reigning love of his or her life.

DENNIS KINLAW, *LET'S START WITH JESUS*

EVENING REFLECTIONS

PSALM 94:14-15, 22—For the LORD will not forsake his people; he will not abandon his heritage; for justice will return to the righteous, and all the upright in heart will follow it . . . The LORD has become my stronghold, and my God the rock of my refuge.

PRAYER—Father, help me to remember you as I fall asleep, and as well think upon you when I am first awakened. You have preserved me from all the dangers of the past day, you support me in trials, and hide me under the shadow of your wings. So let me sleep through this night in your comfort and peace. Amen. *JW*

PSALM 109 ▪ **ISAIAH 4:2-6** ▪ **EPHESIANS 4:1-16** ▪ **MATTHEW 8:28-34**

MORNING MEDITATIONS

PRAYER—O Father, teach me to adore your ways even when I do not understand them. Teach me to be glad that you are my Lord, and to give you thanks for all things, believing that what you have chosen for me is for my best. Give me grace to please you, and then, with an absolute submission to your wisdom, to leave all my concerns in your hands. Amen. **JW**

PSALM 109:21, 26-27—O Lᴏʀᴅ my Lord, act on my behalf for your name's sake; because your steadfast love is good, deliver me . . . Help me, O Lᴏʀᴅ my God! Save me according to your steadfast love. Let them know that this is your hand; you, O Lᴏʀᴅ, have done it.

ISAIAH 4:5, 6b *There Will Be a Refuge and a Shelter*
Then the Lᴏʀᴅ will create over the whole site of Mount Zion and over its places of assembly a cloud by day and smoke and the shining of a flaming fire by night. Indeed over all the glory there will be a canopy . . . a refuge and a shelter from the storm and rain.

EPHESIANS 4:11-13a *Building Up the Body of Christ*
The gifts he gave were that some would be apostles, some prophets, some evangelists, some pastors and teachers, to equip the saints for the work of ministry, for building up the body of Christ, until all of us come to the unity of the faith and of the knowledge of the Son of God.

MATTHEW 8:28-34 *Today's Gospel Reading*

Faith means implicit confidence in Jesus, and that requires not intellect only but a moral giving over of myself to him. How many have really received from God the Spirit that ruled Jesus Christ? . . . The Holy Spirit will bring conviction of sin, he will reveal Jesus Christ, and he will bring in the power.   OSWALD CHAMBERS, *FACING REALITY*

EVENING REFLECTIONS

PSALM 119:142, 144—Your righteousness is an everlasting righteousness, and your law is the truth . . . Your decrees are righteous forever; give me understanding that I may live.

PRAYER—Hear my prayers, O most merciful Father, through the mediation of Jesus Christ our Redeemer, who with you and the Holy Spirit is worshipped and glorified among the saints, one God, blessed forever. Amen. **JW**

**PSALM 105:1-22 ▪ ZECHARIAH 4:1-14 ▪ EPHESIANS 4:17-32 ▪
MATTHEW 9:1-8**

MORNING MEDITATIONS

PRAYER—Eternal God, my Sovereign Lord, I acknowledge all I am, all I have is yours. I humbly thank you for all the blessings you have bestowed upon me—for creating me in your own image, for redeeming me by the death of your blessed Son, and for the assistance of the Holy Spirit, through Christ I pray. Amen. *JW*

PSALM 105:7-8—He is the LORD our God; his judgments are in all the earth. He is mindful of his covenant forever, of the word that he commanded, for a thousand generations.

ZECHARIAH 4:6   *By My Spirit*
"This is the word of the LORD to Zerubbabel: Not by might, nor by power, but by my spirit, says the LORD of hosts."

EPHESIANS 4:30-32   *Do Not Grieve the Holy Spirit*
Do not grieve the Holy Spirit of God, with which you were marked with a seal for the day of redemption. Put away from you all bitterness and wrath and anger . . . and be kind to one another, tenderhearted, forgiving one another, as God in Christ has forgiven you.

MATTHEW 9:1-8   *Today's Gospel Reading*

Christ died to do more for us than get us past the judgment. He died to give us freedom . . . We as sinners must come to realize that we can never atone for our sins . . . We must let the Spirit of holiness cleanse our inner persons as Christians from the defilement of self-interest, realizing this is beyond our capacity to accomplish.

DENNIS KINLAW, *LET'S START WITH JESUS*

EVENING REFLECTIONS

PSALM 105:43-44a, 45—So he brought his people out with joy, his chosen ones with singing. He gave them the lands of the nations . . . that they might keep his statutes and observe his laws. Praise the LORD!

PRAYER—Father, I give you myself and my all; let me look upon myself to have nothing outside of you. Be the sole ruler of life, and when I am tempted to prefer conformity to the world, or the company and customs of those around me, may my answer be, "I am not my own." I am not for myself, nor for the world, but for God alone. God be merciful to your servant. Amen. *JW*

PSALM 102 ▪ JEREMIAH 31:27-34 ▪ EPHESIANS 5:1-20 ▪ MATTHEW 9:9-17

MORNING MEDITATIONS

PRAYER—O Savior of the World, God of God, Light of Light, you are the brightness of your Father's glory. You destroyed the power of the devil and have overcome death. You are my light and my peace. Open my eyes, and fix my gaze on the prize of your high calling, and cleanse my heart of every desire that does not advance your glory. Amen. **JW**

PSALM 102:25-26a, 27—Long ago you laid the foundation of the earth, and the heavens are the work of your hands. They will perish, but you endure; they will all wear out like a garment . . . but you are the same, and your years have no end.

JEREMIAH 31:33   *I Will Put My Law Within Them*
But this is the covenant that I will make with the house of Israel after those days, says the LORD: I will put my law within them, and I will write it on their hearts; and I will be their God, and they shall be my people.

EPHESIANS 5:18b-20   *Be Filled with the Spirit*
Be filled with the Spirit, as you sing psalms and hymns and spiritual songs among yourselves, singing and making melody to the Lord in your hearts, giving thanks to God the Father at all times and for everything in the name of our Lord Jesus Christ.

MATTHEW 9:9-17   *Today's Gospel Reading*

We have been identified with the death of Jesus Christ; our whole life has been invaded by a new spirit. We no longer have any connection with the body of sin, that mystical body that ultimately ends with the devil. Rather, we are made part of the mystical body of Christ by sanctification.   OSWALD CHAMBERS, *BIBLICAL PSYCHOLOGY*

EVENING REFLECTIONS

PSALM 107:21-22—Let them thank the LORD for his steadfast love, for his wonderful works to humankind. And let them offer thanksgiving sacrifices, and tell of his deeds with songs of joy.

PRAYER—Receive me, O my Savior, as a sheep that has gone astray, but is now returned to the great Shepherd of my soul. Accept my imperfect repentance, purify any impurities, fix my instabilities, strengthen my weakness and let your good spirit watch over me always and your love rule in my heart. Amen. **JW**

PSALM 108:1-6 ▪ EZEKIEL 36:22-27 ▪ EPHESIANS 6:10-24 ▪ MATTHEW 9:18-26

MORNING MEDITATIONS

PRAYER—Glory to you, O Blessed Spirit, who comes to us from the Father and the Son. You came down in tongues of fire on the apostles on the first day of the week, enabling them to preach the good news of salvation to a sinful world. Now move in my heart and among your people, as you once moved over the face of the great deep. Bring us all out of that dark chaos into newness of resurrection life, through Christ our Lord. Amen. *JW*

PSALM 108:1, 2b, 5—My heart is steadfast, O God, my heart is steadfast; I will sing and make melody. Awake, my soul! . . . I will awake the dawn . . . Be exalted, O God, above the heavens, and let your glory be over all the earth.

EZEKIEL 36:26-27 *A New Spirit I Will Put Within You*
A new heart I will give you, and a new spirit I will put within you; and I will remove from your body the heart of stone and give you a heart of flesh. I will put my spirit within you, and make you follow my statutes and be careful to observe my ordinances.

EPHESIANS 6:17-18a *Pray in the Spirit*
Take the helmet of salvation, and the sword of the Spirit, which is the word of God. Pray in the Spirit at all times in every prayer and supplication.

MATTHEW 9:18-26 *Today's Gospel Reading*

If we fully face the claims of Scripture about the possibilities of grace, we begin to hunger for that deeper cleansing and filling of God's Spirit, the very Spirit that first shed the love of God within our hearts. To be filled with the Spirit, of course, is to be filled with the very love of God. DENNIS F. KINLAW, *LET'S START WITH JESUS*

EVENING REFLECTIONS

PSALM 33:8-9—Let all the earth fear the LORD; let all the inhabitants of the world stand in awe of him. For he spoke, and it came to be; he commanded, and it stood firm.

PRAYER—Now to God the Father who first loved us, and made us accepted in the Beloved; to God the Son who loved us and washed us from our sins in his own blood; to God the Holy Spirit who spreads the love of God abroad in our hearts, be all love and all glory for time and eternity. Amen! *JW*

PENTECOST SUNDAY

Ashes to Fire Week 14

Sunday: Pentecost: God's Unprofessional Nearness

Read the Gospel passages from John 15:26-27 and 16:4b-15 and the selection from Acts 2:1-21, then read the devotional reflection titled "Pentecost: God's Unprofessional Nearness." Respond to the discussion prompts in the Reflective Journaling section.

THE MUSIC OF ASHES TO FIRE

Week 14: "Fire Deep" (Track 15)

Come, Holy Spirit, Creator Blest
(Veni, Creator Spiritus)

Come, Holy Spirit, Creator blest,
and in our souls take up Your rest;
come with Your grace and heavenly aid
to fill the hearts which You have made.

Now to the Father and the Son,
Who rose from death, be glory given,
with You, O Holy Comforter,
henceforth by all in earth and heaven.

R. Maurus (776–856)

$\mathcal{P}$ENTECOST
God's Unprofessional Nearness

A devotional reflection based on John 15:26-27; 16:4b-15

$\mathcal{R}$ead the Gospel passage first, then the devotional reflection that follows. The discussion prompts at the end will help prepare you for Sunday school and small-group sessions.

Consider the elevator. I don't know who invented it, but he or she obviously didn't appreciate a person's need for space. You know how it goes. The bell rings, the doors open, and two or three people walk into about a four- by six-foot space. The doors automatically close behind them. Now what do they do? First, they get as far away from each other as possible. Then they all face the same way, looking toward the door that has just forced them into this intimacy. They are absolutely transfixed on a series of blinking numbers near the top of this upwardly mobile tin box, as if they fear the thing will skip a floor if they do not watch it carefully. It's an image of our society.

Somehow we have learned that life is safer if you keep a certain distance from people. Some of us are even taught this "professional distance" as part of our workplace training. It is probably necessary to live by the unwritten rules of personal space in at least some relationships. Yet God doesn't seem to know about this. Although many people tend to speak of their relationship to God in terms of distance, God actually doesn't seem to notice. In the Scriptures, God is regularly revealed as One who comes near to us.

This is the conversation Jesus is having with the disciples in chapter 16 of John's Gospel. Here Jesus is teaching that very soon God would come near to them in a new way, nearer to them than they ever imagined possible, nearer than Jesus in his physical presence could be to them. This would happen through the gift of the Holy Spirit.

"Distance." "Nearness." Which of these words best describes God's relation to us? Which of these most accurately describes how you sense God's activity in your life? Distance? Nearness? One of my favorite preachers calls the work of the Holy Spirit in our lives "the unprofessional nearness of God." I suppose all of us struggle at certain times with the question of God's distance or nearness to us. It's an old question. The Hebrews asked it after they had finally broken free from the Pharaoh's captivity and found themselves wandering in the desert. Their difficult journey had them often asking, "Is the Lord with us or not?"

It's still our question. Is the Lord near or far? When I am on the brink of losing my job and I'm worried sick over how to provide for my family, is God really involved in that? Does God really know what I am dealing with? Does God really care about me and the things I am worried about? Our minds may tell us, "Yes, God is near; the Lord promised never to leave us." The challenge is that in the trials of life we can easily begin to feel the distance more than the nearness.

Jesus knew this would happen. He knew that unless we could truly know and experience the nearness of God in a sure way, it would be easy for us to assume that God had become professionally distant. As we come near the end of John's Gospel then, Jesus begins to teach his disciples about how God will come near in the person of the Holy Spirit. Jesus has much to say about the work of the Spirit in our lives, but in this text he focused on a particular aspect of the Spirit's work that may be a meaningful word to those of us who find ourselves wondering at times just how involved God really is in our lives.

Jesus says, "When the Spirit of truth comes, he will guide you into all the truth" (John 16:13). We tend to think of truth as something that is "out there" somewhere and we have to get to it. It is the knowledge and wisdom for what life is really all about and how we should live it. Yet we have this sense that truth is something we have to work very hard to attain, that we must be especially astute to find it.

Perhaps we think of discipleship in this way. We picture ourselves trying to learn to be nearer to God, as if somehow we have to overcome the distance we have to find God. Our spiritual journey may indeed seem to us as if we are walking toward God, seeking God. The truth is, God has already come very close because he wants to walk with us. Yet Jesus refers to the Spirit as our Guide and Teacher. Now, through the death and resurrection of Jesus Christ, God has come, through the outpouring of the Spirit, not just to walk with us on this earth as Jesus did, but actually to dwell in our hearts.

What good news! Think about the implications. The truth into which the Holy Spirit guides us is not simply some kind of rational understanding of the precepts of Christianity. Jesus is talking about an intimate knowledge and experience of God, so that the life of Christ becomes our life. In other words, the role of the Holy Spirit in our lives is about much more than teaching us ideas we need to know. The Spirit forms the very life of Christ in us.

In the next chapter of John we hear Jesus praying for his disciples. He prays, Father, "sanctify them in the truth" (17:17), which we no doubt need to hear in light of the previous declaration of Jesus, "I am . . . the truth" (14:6). Do you see what Jesus is teaching? Our God is not one who is off in a distant heaven looking down on us like some kind of ant farm wondering why we are all running around so. Our Father is not a God of distance but of nearness, coming near to us in the presence of the Holy Spirit, living in us to make us his holy children.

Which perhaps begs the question, "Is your relationship with God better described by distance or by nearness? Do you know the peace and joy of being led by the Spirit? Are you experiencing the unprofessional nearness of God? If not, would you be willing to accept the possibility that the distance is your responsibility?" "Draw near to God, and he will draw near to you" (James 4:8) is the helpful word. This encouragement from James is not a condition to be met before God will come near. It is instead a beautiful invitation to realize that God was never distant. That's the joyful news of Pentecost. —JR

After reading the passage from John 15:26-27;
16:4b-15 and the devotional reflection "Pentecost:
God's Unprofessional Nearness," you may also want
to read the following related passages:
Acts 2:1-21; Psalm 104:24-34, 35b; Romans 8:22-27

The discussion prompts that follow will help prepare you to participate in your Sunday school class or small-group study. Use your Reflective Journaling section to record any other insights that come to you as you read the Gospel lesson and the devotional reflection.

DISCUSSION PROMPT NO. 1: JOHN 15 AND 16

Describe the relationship of the Trinity—Father, Son, and Holy Spirit—in this passage.

DISCUSSION PROMPT NO. 2: JOHN 15 AND 16

Why did Jesus consider it better for the disciples to have the Holy Spirit with them than for him to be present with them in person?

DISCUSSION PROMPT NO. 3: JOHN 15 AND 16

Describe the relationship between the Holy Spirit and the apostles. Do Christians today experience a relationship with the Holy Spirit in the same way? Explain.

DISCUSSION PROMPT NO. 4: JOHN 15 AND 16

In John 16:12-13 Jesus indicates that the Holy Spirit will teach the Church on his behalf once he is gone. Give some examples from the New Testament.

DISCUSSION PROMPT NO. 5: DEVOTIONAL REFLECTION

Think about the writer's question: "Is your relationship with God better described by distance or by nearness?" Do some Reflective Journaling on the answer to this question.

REFLECTIVE JOURNALING

_____

_____

_____

_____

_____

_____

_____

_____

_____

_____

_____

_____

_____

_____

SOURCES

Chambers, Oswald. *Faith: A Holy Walk.* Grand Rapids: Discovery House, 1999.

Devotional reflection for Ascension Sunday (Easter Season—Week Seven), "A Holy Church," by Jeren Rowell, was originally published in the *Preacher's Magazine*, November 18, 2007. http://www.nazarenepreacher.com/articles/36-sermons/736-a-holy -church (accessed July 22, 2011).

From the Father's to Churches, Edited by Brother Kenneth. London: William Collins, Sons and Co., 1987.

Kelly, Thomas R. *A Testament of Devotion.* New York: Harper and Row Publishers, 1941.

Kinlaw, Dennis. *Let's Start with Jesus.* Grand Rapids: Zondervan, 2005.

Lewis, C. S. *The Joyful Christian.* New York: Macmillan Publishing Company, 1977.

Munro, Bertha. *Truth for Today.* Kansas City: Beacon Hill Press, 1958.

Nouwen, Henri J. M. *With Burning Hearts.* New York: Orbis Books, 1995.

Phillips, J. B. *Ring of Truth.* New York: The Macmillan Company, 1967.

Ratzinger, Joseph. *Jesus of Nazareth.* San Francisco: Ignatius Press, 2011.

Sayers, Dorothy. *Creed or Chaos?* Manchester, N.H.: Sophia Institute Press, 1949.

Welch, Reuben. *Preaching from 2 Corinthians 3 through 5.* Kansas City: Beacon Hill Press of Kansas City, 1988.

Wesley, John. *A Collection of Forms of Prayer for Every Day in the Week.* Nashville: United Methodist Publishing House, 1992.